Praise for *Your Keys to Moving On*

"When women come to us grappling with divorce, one of their greatest fears is what will happen to them and their beloved "home"?

After all, as women we have put so much into our nest. We've dreamed about it, worked for it, feathered and decorated it, and often raised a family there. It's part of of who we are! An identity. But it's an emotional relationship. Here's a book that helps you move out of that fear of what change would mean by helping you take action and investigate what the real value of your home is. This is a great resource and workbook for teasing apart the question of 'What should one do?'"

—LIZA CALDWELL,
Divorce Recovery and Leadership Coach, SAS for Women™ Cofounder

"Joan's book is must read resource for families going through divorce and having to deal with emotional and financial decisions relative to their home. She addresses the often misunderstood and challenging topic of real estate through her expertise and experience. Joan is a valued and trusted professional on *LifeThruDivorce.com* and we highly recommend Joan's book to guide you through all the decisions you need to understand during and after your divorce journey."

—PERRI TEITELBAUM, MICHELLE ZUDECK
and PAM PEREIRA, Founders
www.LifeThruDivorce.com

Your Keys to Moving On

A Guide to Navigating Divorce and the Marital Home

Joan Rogliano
as seen on **TODAY**

Your Keys to Moving On
© Copyright 2017, Joan Rogliano.
All rights reserved.

No part of this book may be reproduced or distributed in any form or by any means (written, electronic, mechanical, recording, photocopy or otherwise) or stored in a database or retrieval system, without the prior written permission of the author or publisher, except in the case of brief quotations embodied in critical articles and reviews.

Disclaimer: The author has changed the client's name in all case studies throughout this book to protect clients' privacy.

Books may be purchased in quantity and/or for special sales by contacting the publisher or author at her email address:
joan@roglianorealestategroup.com

Cover and Interior Design: Rebecca Finkel, F + P Graphic Design
Editing: Barbara McNichol Editorial

Library of Congress Number: 2017905490
ISBN: (print book) 978-0-9988511-0-5
(e-book) 978-0-9988511-1-2

First Edition
Printed in USA

To Doug and Jennifer

When I was 5 years old, my mother always told me that happiness was the key to life. When I went to school, they asked me what I wanted to be when I grew up. I wrote down "happy." They told me I didn't understand the assignment, and I told them they didn't understand life.

— John Lennon

Before We Begin…

Divorce is a word that brings discomfort to many people. Yet it also connects us, as most everyone knows someone who has been through a divorce.

Most couples are unprepared to navigate this thorny path of divorce, which can be devastating. Being thrust into one of the most vulnerable experiences of life and then faced with the stress of selling the family home, this refrain is frequently repeated: "I realize now I didn't know what I didn't know." It's crucial for both parties involved to remain vigilant as they arm themselves with information so they can make the best decisions for themselves and their families.

The best plan, of course, is to have a plan, and that's what *Your Keys to Moving On* provides. Because divorce becomes a business transaction in many respects, this book hands you the keys to create a customized strategy that works for everyone.

Divorce takes a team of professionals to ensure the right decisions are made the first time. After all, no one wants the expense and emotional turmoil of post-divorce decree litigation. That's why it's essential for you to assemble a team of professionals who will truly advocate for you, understand your family's needs, and work diligently within their area of expertise. They must be team players who agree to collaborate with one another toward your goals—and put the focus on *you*!

Most divorcing couples recognize a need for a certain level of legal guidance, which could take the form of mediation, collaboration, or full-course litigation. Other team members should include a Realtor®, loan originator, financial planner, tax adviser, and perhaps a counselor or therapist.

Outside of arrangements for children, the disposition of the marital home during a divorce remains one of the most agonizing challenges for couples. For most, home represents more than a roof over their heads. It is their refuge from the world, the hearth in which they raise their children, and the sanctuary where key moments of family life have played out. Home represents both financial and emotional stability, making it more than a stated asset on the divorcing couple's balance sheet. Indeed, when a divorce is imminent, a family home can become a lightning rod for charged feelings and volatility.

Frequently a Realtor® receives the first call from a divorcing couple. People want to be assured they'll have a roof over their heads, particularly when children are involved. Do they have the option to keep the family home? Do they have to sell the house quickly to wipe the state clean and move on? At this time more than ever, most couples aren't aware they have choices and should explore them fully before making a decision.

It's never wise to take real estate advice from well-meaning family members, friends, or other professionals. Real estate remains a local specialty, particularly in our mercurial national market. A full-time local Realtor® is needed to provide professional guidance.

If You're Divorcing . . .

When it comes to divorce and real estate, you have three options regarding your home:

1. Sell the home and divide the profits as agreed.

2. One spouse buys out the other spouse's interest.

3. One party stays in the home for a specified period of time and then the home is sold.

As you face these choices, you need solid real estate guidance regarding the pros and cons as you answer these common questions:

1. Is it possible to buy a new home prior to the finalization of the divorce?

2. What if one party owned the home prior to the marriage?

3. What are the possible tax consequences if one party keeps the home?

4. If one party is buying the other out, is it always advisable to have an inspection done prior to the purchase?

5. What are the pitfalls if one party remains in the home and both parties remain on the mortgage?

6. What are possible dangers if one party remains in the home but is not on the mortgage?

This book holds the key to your choices and helps you explore the options as you move forward with your divorce. It also offers financing strategies that can enable you to keep your home as well as explore the pros and cons of renting versus buying a new place to call home.

Should you decide that moving to a new home is your best bet, look for the step-by-step overview of the home-buying process. Be sure to use the financial tools in this book to help you gather essential information as you set your immediate and long-term goals.

Most important, the information you find here can provide you with peace of mind. Throughout this difficult time, you can empower yourself with knowledge to achieve the best outcome for you and your family.

Remember, you are not in this alone. It would be a privilege to serve you as you chart your course for the future.

— Joan Rogliano

Contents

CHAPTER ONE Your First Steps to Moving On 17
   Make the Right Decision for YOU
      about the Marital Home 17
   Resist Outside Pressures 18
   Minimizing Disruption... 19
   Choosing a Home That Reflects the New "You".......... 20
   Deciding to Buy or Rent....................................... 22
   Are You Ready to Own?.. 23

CHAPTER TWO Your Financial Picture 29
   Are You Prepared for Homeownership? 29
   What's Your Comfort Level?.................................. 30
   Taking Control of Your Finances 31
   Understand Your Credit History 32
   Know Your Credit Score.. 33
   What Goes into Your Credit Score?........................ 34
   How to Improve Your Credit Score 36
   The Perils of Joint Accounts 37
   How to Build Your Credit History 39

CHAPTER THREE How to Finance Your Home Purchase ... 45
   Traditional Lending Sources 45
   Federal Housing Authority 46
   Reverse Mortgages... 46

Veterans Administration Programs 47
Fannie Mae and Freddie Mac Programs 48
Non-Government-Backed Loans 49
The Cost of Your Loan 50
Interest Rate vs. Annual Percentage Rate (APR) 51
Choosing a Loan Originator 52
Strategies to Refinance Your Existing Home 52
Home Equity Line of Credit (HELOC) 54
Creating Your Own Solution 55
What Lenders Need from Buyers 55

CHAPTER FOUR The Real Estate Buy/Sell Process 61
Selling Your Home 61
Home Selling Checklist 62
Make Your Dream Home a Reality 63
Finding a House on Your Own 64
For Sale By Owners (FSBOs) 65
Public Home Search Wedsites 66
Find the Right Realtor® 66
Professional Credentials 68
Agency Representation vs. Transaction Broker 68
Pre-Qualified vs. Pre-Approved 69
Offer to Purchase Process 70
Contract Contingencies 71
Title Search and Title Insurance 72
Home Inspections 74
Appraisal Process 76
Home Warranty 77
Title Tranfer 79

CHAPTER FIVE Your Personal Workbook 83
    Financial Overview 84
    Family Budget 85
    Mortgage Calculator 89
    Employment History 90
    Moving Expenses Worksheet 93
    Liabilities 94
    Assets 100
    Net Worth Summary....................................... 117

Glossary 121
Resources 143
Acknowledgments 147
Wildflower Group 148
About the Author 149

Single is not a status, it is a word that describes a person who is strong enough to live and enjoy life without depending on others.

— Anonymous

CHAPTER ONE

Your First Steps to Moving On

A home is so much more than a roof over our heads. For many, our homes are the foundation of our family life and a safe harbor where we retreat from the demands of the world. As a result, a forced sale of the home can be an emotionally (not to mention financially) wrenching experience.

Make the Right Decision for YOU about the Marital Home

Yet while if feels like you're being pressured to make a decision you may not want to make, you do have options. It's imperative to understand the choices available as well as your motivation for deciding on your course of action. Here are the three main options:

   1. **Both parties sell the marital home.** If there is equity in it, they split that amount in an agreed-upon way. This allows both parties to move forward with no connection to each other regarding this real estate asset.

   2. **One spouse purchases the home from the other.** An often-overlooked cost with this option could be paying capital gains tax for the person who retains the home. Married couples are entitled to a $500,000 capital gains

tax exemption while a single person is allowed a $250,000 tax exemption. Given the high real estate appreciation in certain areas, this may create an unwanted tax burden when the home is ultimately sold.

3. **The divorce agreement states one party will remain in the house** for a specified time and then it will be sold. People frequently use this option when a child is close to finishing school or one party has a specific reason to stay in the marital home for a while. Because the current mortgage remains in place, both parties are still in an ownership position and responsible for the mortgage payment, which can be problematic. This option can also prohibit a new home purchase for the person moving out because of setting up a debt-to-income ratio that's too high to qualify for a new mortgage. It also leaves the person moving in a vulnerable position. For example, s/he must rely on the other person to be responsible for maintaining the home's condition, keeping up with the landscaping, and making sure the property retains its value. With this scenario, the final agreement must be carefully thought through.

Resisting Outside Pressures

When you're in the midst of a divorce, it may seem like those around you suggest you immediately take action regarding your house. Remember, there's usually time to take a deep breath so you can educate yourself on your choices and the ramifications for each before choosing your direction. People can be well meaning, but ultimately this is your decision to make.

Don't be intimidated by others or by the magnitude of this decision; instead, rely on your trusted team. Consult with your real estate and mortgage advisors as well as legal, financial, and tax advisors to carefully assess local real estate market conditions and the advantages to you should you sell or stay. They can help you understand that your ultimate choice fits with your new lifestyle, budget, and goals.

Minimizing Disruption
Concern About Your Children
If you have children at home, no one needs to tell you they'll experience your divorce as a major event in their lives. Because they have plenty to contend with as they come to terms with family changes, the challenge of moving to a new home can add to their concerns. A move could involve a shift in their social circle, a disruption in their routine, and a change in schools. If possible, allowing them to stay in their home even temporarily gives them a sense of continuity and security during a time of great emotional upheaval.

Concern About Yourself
Children are not the only ones who experience divorce as a time of distress. Even amicable divorces can take an emotional toll on you. Your past social and interpersonal relationships may change, and you'll be growing into new roles. In the best of circumstances, these personal changes can be a lot to manage. Add to that the task of selling your existing home and finding a new one, and you could have the ingredients for emotional overload.

Also, keep in mind how your social network will play a vital part in helping you weather the current storm. Leaving behind friends and neighbors you've come to depend on can deprive you of your support system just when you need it most. Give yourself breathing space as much as you can.

Timing the Sale for the Best Price

The timing of your home sale can greatly influence how quickly it sells and at what price. Choosing your time wisely can minimize the length of time your home is on the market and, in effect, increase your sale price. In contrast, if your divorce forces you to sell immediately, you may have no choice but to accept what you can get for your home in a less than ideal market.

If you decide that moving is the best choice, consult with your Realtor® about market conditions and plan accordingly. Rushing to action may not be wise.

Protecting Your Lifestyle

For some people, the task of finding a new home equal to their existing home can be difficult or impossible. Following a divorce, most people face a reduction in income and, according to Lenore Weitzman's book *The Divorce Revolution,* a typical woman in the U.S. experiences a 73 percent reduction in her standard of living after a divorce.

The tools in this book are key to understanding what your financial position will be post-divorce. The budget programs will help you take charge as you create a "new normal" for your life and your finances. Be sure to work through the exercises in Chapter Five to understand your financial position accurately.

Choosing a Home That Reflects the New "You"

You may find your existing home no longer fits the lifestyle and personality of the new "you." Your current community may no longer suit you, while other housing options could become more appealing to you. A divorce provides a chance to travel new paths and create different priorities through fresh options. For example, a house on large grounds that requires extensive outdoor maintenance may no longer be desirable compared to a townhome with no exterior maintenance. You may want to relocate to take advantage of new social opportunities. If your new status requires you to work outside the home, relocating could minimize your daily commute to work and/or child care arrangements.

Tread Carefully with Emotional Decisions
Of course for some, the best medicine after divorce is to get as far away as possible from the marital home. A new place to live might seem like just the cure for a case of bad memories and high financial overhead.

Yet many who made a quick decision to leave their marital home as a short-term cure for bad memories came to regret this course of action. In some cases, money was lost as a result of their "fire sale" approach to disposing of the unwanted property. In other cases, positive feelings about their home prevailed over time. Remember, moving is a *financial* decision as well as an *emotional* one.

Consider Your Options
If you feel you want nothing more than to close the door on your home forever, consider alternatives that might suit you better. For example, you could lease an apartment and rent your home to someone else. This action provides time and distance to sort through your feelings. Then when the time is right, you can decide if your home is the best spot for you. If it isn't, you'd put it on the market when you're in the best position to get the price you deserve. More important, you want to feel reassured you gave this major decision due consideration. If, on the other hand, you have a change of heart about selling your home, then you can move back in!

One Big Advantage of Owning a Home

Tax breaks! The U.S. federal government allows homeowners to deduct not only their interest expenses on a first mortgage but also some loan and settlement costs. For example, if you pay $12,000 a year in interest on your mortgage, then $12,000 of that amount might be applied against your net income to reduce your tax liability. Be sure to consult your tax advisor.

Renters do *not* have access to similar tax breaks. **For detailed information, check these IRS Publications at https://www.irs.gov/publications/.**

- 936 Home Mortgage Interest Deduction
- 521 Moving Expenses
- 523 Selling Your Home
- 908 Bankruptcy Tax Guide
- 530 First Time Homebuyers

(You'll also find them listed in Resources at the back of this book.)

Deciding to Buy or Rent

Yes, emotions will be high during this transition. It's critical to strongly consider the option of selling your existing home, banking your share of the proceeds, and moving into a rental before making long-term decisions about your housing. Study the pros and cons of renting versus owning in Figure 1.1 and see what fits your situation best.

Note: For a clear picture of the financial advantages to owning your own home, visit: **http://www.ginniemae.gov/rent_vs_buy/rent_vs_buy_calc.asp?section=Search.**

There, you can compare the financial impact of renting versus buying based on the amount of rent you would pay, the amount of your mortgage, down payment, length of mortgage, and other factors.

Home Ownership	Rent or Lease
Potentially large initial investment	Smaller initial investment
Control over your space	No control
Stable monthly payments	Subject to change
Maintenance and repair	Covered by landlord
Tax incentives	None
Building home equity	None
Less mobility	Short-term commitment
Risk of loss	Risk of eviction
Insurance costs	Slight
For a clear picture of the financial advantages to owning your own home, visit http://www.ginniemae.gov/rent_vs_buy/rent_vs_buy_calc.asp?section=Search. You will have the opportunity to compare the financial impact of renting versus buying based on the amount of rent you would pay, the amount of your mortgage, down payment, length of mortgage, and other factors.	

Figure 1.1

Buying a home is a decision you can't take lightly for financial reasons alone. Consider your comfort with making a long-term financial commitment of this magnitude during your divorce proceedings. It is often wise to think of your next housing choice as an interim stop. Finding a rental for six months or a year can buy time for your thoughts and priorities to crystallize before again taking the plunge to home ownership.

Are You Ready to Own?

You have many decisions ahead in your divorce process. Having a picture of where you'll be living can help you feel stronger about all other decisions you have to make. Your answers to the following questions guide you to make that all-important first decision. So take a deep breath, relax, and gather the facts as you see how well prepared you are to be a home owner.

☐ **Yes** ☐ **No** Do you have a steady source of income that will cover all the expenses of home ownership?

☐ **Yes** ☐ **No** Are you comfortable with the idea of staying in one place for the next few years?

☐ **Yes** ☐ **No** Is your family situation stable, with no planned changes in your family's composition over the next few years?

☐ **Yes** ☐ **No** Can you take responsibility for home repairs and maintenance even if you have to hire others to do the work?

☐ **Yes** ☐ **No** Do you have access to funds for earnest money, a down payment, and other home purchase costs such as closing costs and settlement fees?

☐ **Yes** ☐ **No** Will permanent housing meet your social, lifestyle, and commuting needs for the next few years?

☐ **Yes** ☐ **No** If you need to sell your existing home before buying a new home, are you willing to undertake the investment in getting your home "sale ready"?

☐ **Yes** ☐ **No** Is now a good time to change your children's environment?

The more "yes" answers you provided to the questions above, the more likely home ownership is the right option for you. But if "no" answers dominate, then it's a sign to consider alternatives other than home ownership.

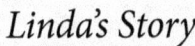

Linda's Story

Linda consulted with her divorce team to accomplish her goal regarding her home. She wanted to stay in the home she called her "dream home in the foothills." She had an excellent employment history but wanted to improve her credit, which required a novel approach.

At the time of the divorce, the home had a certain amount of equity built up, so she was counseled to take her share of the equity as part of the refinance process. She used the equity money to pay off her credit cards that had high monthly payments. This helped lower her debt-to-income ratio and increased her credit score.

Linda remained in the marital home for a few years and then decided to enhance her new lifestyle by moving to an urban location. By taking her time and weighing her options carefully, Linda enjoyed living in her dream home a little longer, minimized the stress of moving on and improved her credit score in the process.

Sometimes good things fall apart so better things can fall together.

—Marilyn Monroe

CHAPTER TWO

Your Financial Picture

Once you have answered the question about whether you are emotionally ready for home ownership, the next critical question asks if you're financially prepared.

Are You Prepared for Home Ownership?

Home ownership is a major financial commitment. In fact, for most consumers, their home is the single largest financial purchase they will ever undertake. Not only does a home purchase dictate your lifestyle choices for years to come, it also dramatically shapes how you spend money in the future.

Home ownership involves more than making monthly mortgage payments. Here is a list of only some of the financial obligations that go hand-in-hand with home ownership:

- Mortgage expense (principal and interest)
- Utilities
- Annual maintenance, repair (approximately 1% of the home's value)
- Homeowner's insurance
- Mortgage insurance
- Property taxes
- Homeowners Association fees

Combined, all of these expenses can quickly add up, yet they should not exceed a certain percentage of your gross income. That percentage, which is different for everyone, is determined by your income, credit history, and credit score.

In years past, loan originators required all home ownership expenses to represent no more than 28 percent of total gross income. However, with the surge in home values, that ratio has gone up. To get approved for a mortgage, lenders are permitting housing expenses to take a significantly higher percent of gross income. That's why it's important to talk to your loan originator about your situation and determine what ratios are allowed to refinance your present home or purchase a new one. After reviewing the numbers carefully, evaluate your budget and personal choices. As you do, consider financial guidelines as simply that: guidelines. Once you know the financial benchmarks the industry considers appropriate, the only person who can tell you what feels right is you!

Note: Know that you won't be able to get a loan until your divorce is final. Loans cannot be made to anyone involved in a legal proceeding, and a divorce is a legal proceeding.

What is Your Comfort Level?

There can be a world of difference between what a spreadsheet says you can afford and your comfort level. Many people avoid having a large portion of their monthly income committed for housing. They prefer not to be "house poor," which means tying up too much of their total income to keep a roof over their heads. Instead, they like the freedom of spending money on other priorities such as travel, entertainment, or investments.

If the assessment reveals you are qualified for a higher purchase price than you thought possible, good for you. It doesn't mean you need to spend that much; perhaps a more conservative approach works better for you. If you want to spend more or less than the guidelines suggest, work with your Realtor® to find a home in your price range that meets your financial needs as well as your lifestyle and emotional needs.

Remember, with your new status, you have three main options. You could buy a home that fits your needs, refinance your present home, or choose to rent. The choice is yours.

Taking Control of Your Finances

Where do you start to assess your financial picture? This might be an overwhelming thought. Perhaps you keep an accurate financial picture or monthly accounting of your income sources with a software program such as Quicken. That way, the information you need will be at your fingertips.

If you have not kept accurate records in the past, that's fine, but you need to tackle this task now. While it might be an overwhelming thought, Chapter Five walks you through the process of creating a financial overview. It also features a short list of information a loan originator will need if you choose to refinance your present home or finance a new home purchase.

Don't stress out about creating a system to handle your finances. To assess your financial picture, choose a program that helps you determine your spending and will encourage you to keep up with your monthly accounting.

The following programs are economical, easy to use, and empowering!

- *Quicken from Intuit*
- *www.mint.com*
- *http://moneydance.com/*

- *www.mvelopes.com*
- *www.budgetpulse.com*

(You'll also find these listed in Resources at the back of this book.)

Once you're ready for a refinance or new purchase and have determined you have the income to reach your goal, your next step to getting a loan is a credit assessment. Your credit history and credit score will determine your eligibility. And if you decide home ownership isn't in your current plan, it's still valuable to know your credit numbers.

Understand Your Credit History

In today's high-tech world, creditors nearly instantaneously report your credit activities to the three major credit reporting agencies. These agencies provide your credit history when requested by any potential or existing creditors. Under U.S. federal law, all three credit reporting agencies are required to give you one free credit report a year. One approach would be to check with one agency in January, one in April, and the third in August. This gives you an ongoing picture of your credit. You can request your free report by contacting the firms directly at:

- Equifax *www.econsumer.equifax.com*
- Experian *www.experian.com/consumer*
- Transunion *www.transunion.com/consumer*

Alternatively, you can request free credit reports from all three agencies simultaneously from *www.annualcreditreport.com*. (You'll also find these listed in Resources at the back of this book.)

Note: It's imperative you check your credit at least annually. Why? Frequently, mistakes are caught or repairs needed that can take four to six weeks to fix and another 30 to 60 days to be reflected by the credit agencies. You play a key role in keeping the reports accurate, so be proactive about keeping your scores up-to-date.

Know Your Credit Score

Credit history is only part of the story, however. To know how favorably your finances will be viewed by a potential lender, find out your actual credit score. See Figure 2.1, which shows how credit scores stack up for various percentages of the U.S. population of homeowners. You can obtain your score for a small fee from *www.myfico.com*. (At the time of publication, *myfico.com* charged $19.95 per person for that service.)

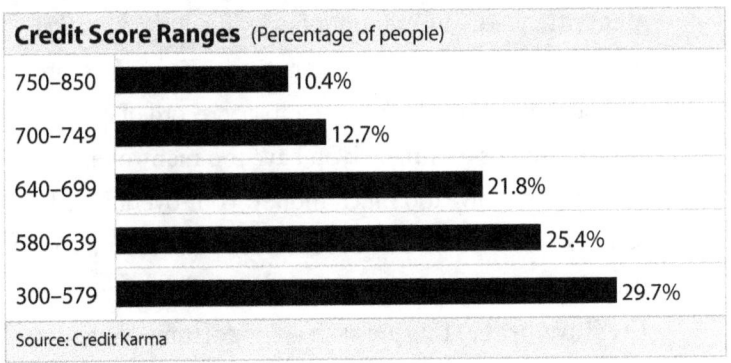

Figure 2.1

Lending institutions may use your credit report, a credit score, or both to determine if you are a good financial risk as a borrower. In general, you're better off if your score is above 620 because a higher score gives you greater borrowing power. If your score falls below 620, you would be considered a high-risk borrower and assessed higher interest charges than others. In fact, you might have difficulty finding a loan program altogether.

See Figure 2.2 to see how your credit score affects the amount of interest charged for mortgage loans.

How a Credit Score Affects a Loan's Interest Rate

Credit Score	Available Interest Rate
720–850	5.00%
700–719	5.25%
675–699	5.50%
620–674	6.375%
619 and below	Not applicable

FICO launched a new site to help consumers understand their credit. Visit **www.scoreinfo.org**.

Figure 2.2

What Goes Into Your Score?

A credit score is a snapshot of your past financial behavior. Among the factors that credit scoring entities consider are:

- **Amounts owed:** The amount of overall debt is a particularly important factor in determining your credit score. Although you could have an exemplary record of making your payments on time, if you have too many open accounts and owe too much money, your overall credit score will be low. If you have several open accounts with zero balances, your credit score may be adversely affected. Creditors believe this presents an opportunity to go into greater debt.

- **Your payment history:** If you consistently make your payments on time, your score will be better than if you have late payments. Be aware that being delinquent for 90 days or more will significantly lower your score.

- **Public records about your financial history:** Public records will include any bankruptcy filings you have as well as judgments, liens, lawsuits, wage attachments, and collection agency action taken against you. Any of these events can lower your credit score substantially.

- **New credit:** Your recent credit activity is closely scrutinized. If you have suddenly opened several new accounts, the scoring agencies could consider this a warning sign. It provides the ability to take on larger debt. On the plus side, however, re-establishing a positive credit history with a creditor with whom you have had past payment problems will work to your advantage.
- **Length of credit history:** Those who have a long credit history are able to give the scoring agency a better overall picture of their financial history than those with a short credit history.
- **Types of credit:** The scoring agencies look at the types of debt you carry, including department store accounts, credit card accounts, auto loans, and student loans.

The illustration in Figure 2.3 shows how myfico and other scoring agencies create your score.

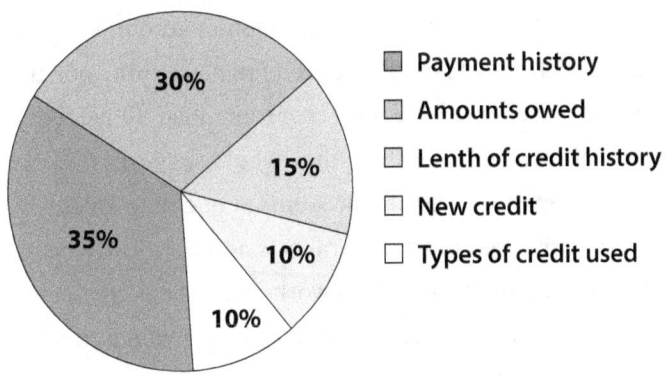

Figure 2.3

How to Improve Your Credit Score

Good news. If your score is less than you'd like it to be (frequently true when going through a divorce), don't despair. You can make improvements to repair it. Consult with a loan originator for tips and then be patient with yourself. It takes time to make changes and then more time for credit reporting agencies to reflect any improvement.

Here are specific tips to improve your credit score:

- **Pay your bills on time:** If you have gotten behind, get current. The longer your history of on-time payments, the stronger your credit will be. If you pay less than the amount due—even if you make the partial payments on time—your account will be considered "past due."

- **Pay down your debt:** The larger the amount of your outstanding debt, the lower your score. If possible, pay off those high account balances and strive to keep balances low in the future.

Note: If you're in the midst of a divorce, proceed with care. Temporary orders might limit what you can and can't do with any joint accounts. Before you close or pay off joint accounts, be sure to discuss it with your team of legal and financial professionals.

Credit counselors advise not using more than 30 percent of your available credit. In addition, they would suggest:

- **Do not open several new accounts at one time unless you really need them.** Several new accounts lower your average account age, which works against a higher credit score. It also raises a red flag to a creditor wondering about your long-term intentions to take on more debt.

- **Do not close unused credit cards just to raise your credit score.** Doing this will not have an immediate impact, and you might need this additional credit in the future.

- **Do not use one credit card to pay off another.** Pay off your cards one at a time if necessary. You can owe the same amount of money to fewer lenders and actually have a higher credit score.

- **Re-establish your credit.** If you've had trouble with a past creditor but have rectified the situation, open a new account. This can definitely help your credit history.

- **Realize that negative credit events** stay on your credit history for a while. These events include action taken by a collection agency, a bankruptcy, or a foreclosure. The length of time it remains on your credit report is determined by the type of action taken, even if you have paid off the debt or are now current with your payments.

- **Know that closing an account does not remove it from your credit history.** Even a closed account can be used to calculate your credit score.

- **Be optimistic!** Most creditors want to help you improve your situation, so don't hesitate to contact them and ask for their cooperation and guidance.

The Perils of Joint Accounts

Statistics show that women experience a more extreme reduction in their financial position than men after divorce. According to the U.S. Census Bureau, in five out of six cases women become the custodial parent for the children. Among dual income families, statistics show that women earn less than their spouses in two-thirds of the families.

Based on this powerful information, we want to encourage women in particular to become aware of their financial matters in detail.

Today, increasingly more women understand the importance of building a credit history in their own name. It's recommended that, whenever possible, each party open a credit account in his or her name. This provides a woman with an individual account in case of divorce or her spouse's death. It also provides an uninterrupted credit history as well as access to credit.

If all your credit accounts are held jointly in both your name and your spouse's, you will both share equally in the credit history of that account. If you and your spouse used the account responsibly and made your payments on time, then you'll share in the positive credit history you have created together.

Unfortunately, after divorce or a spouse's death, each creditor will assess your income and decide whether or not to grant you a new line of credit in your own name. In some situations, individuals had an exemplary payment record with a creditor on a joint account but were unable to open an account with that creditor in their own name. Why? They didn't have sufficient income! Alternatively, the creditor may allow you to open an account in your own name, but the credit line could be substantially less than expected or needed as the amount depends on income.

Word to the Wise: You can't avoid having your credit re-evaluated by not telling the creditors you and your spouse are no longer married. When you're divorcing, you don't want to be jointly responsible for a line of credit or any other debt. You have probably heard horror stories about abuse when joint accounts were not frozen or closed at the time of divorce.

Note: As mentioned earlier, proceed with caution toward joint accounts if you and your spouse are in the process of dissolving your marriage. If your orders are temporary, these may limit what you can and cannot do with joint accounts. *Before you close accounts or pay off account balances, seek professional guidance from your legal, tax, and financial advisors.*

How to Build Your Credit History

To begin building a credit history, follow these essential tips:

- **DO apply for credit accounts in your own name but only as needed.** Someone with no credit history will often have a much lower credit score than someone who does, even if that credit history isn't spotless. Remember, opening several new accounts at once can actually lower your credit score.

- **DO use your accounts wisely.** That usually means making charges to your account and paying them off quickly. Those in the credit-granting industry call people who pay off their entire balance every month "dead beats"! It's because these consumers pay off their balances before the creditor can impose finance charges, their major source of income. Some credit reporting agencies won't even consider these timely balance-in-full payments in a consumer's credit history. So while you're establishing your good credit history, consider opening a low interest account you can pay off in about six months.

- **DO research both your credit score and credit history annually.** Errors in reporting details are common, and the longer misinformation stays on your report, the harder it can be to remove. Conducting this review keeps you updated on how your credit is being viewed by potential lenders. Take this time to address any deficiencies before you apply for a loan.

Note: Credit reporting agencies often take four to six weeks to fix errors. So if you're applying for credit in the near future, make checking your credit history your first step. Then correct any errors before a lender investigates your standing.

- **If you have debts you cannot pay, contact an organization affiliated with the National Foundation for Credit Counseling.** People in these organizations work with your creditors to help avoid late fees and reduce interest rates. If your creditors agree and you make your payments on time, your credit report won't suffer lasting damage. Visit this website for more information: **https://www.nfcc.org.**

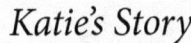

Katie's Story

Like many of her peers, Katie Dobson left the workforce and a lucrative career when she and her husband started their family. While their two children were still young, Katie and her husband decided to divorce. Determined to maintain a good lifestyle for her two young children, Katie knew that would mean moving from her isolated mountain community to a neighborhood close to her work.

But first, Katie and her husband needed to sell the home they had shared.

When their house finally went under contract, the buyer was to take possession in only three weeks. Katie had no choice except to make an interim move to a friend's cabin. This move gave her time to find a cute place in town near good schools and only minutes from her work. While not her dream home, it was well suited to her immediate needs.

Although Katie had a good job, she had little recent employment history and couldn't yet use her spousal maintenance or child support to qualify for a loan. With nothing left from the sale of her marital home to help her buy a new one, Katie needed assistance both financing her mortgage and finding a source for the down payment. The loan originator found Katie a low-cost down payment loan, and a local Housing Finance Authority gave her a second loan so she could pay a three percent down payment. As Katie's paycheck and spousal maintenance history was established, she was able to totally pay off her second mortgage. She then refinanced the first mortgage at an even lower interest rate.

Today, Katie and her two high-school-age kids live in a larger home than the first one she bought after the divorce. Their first home has become rental property, adding extra income to her household each month.

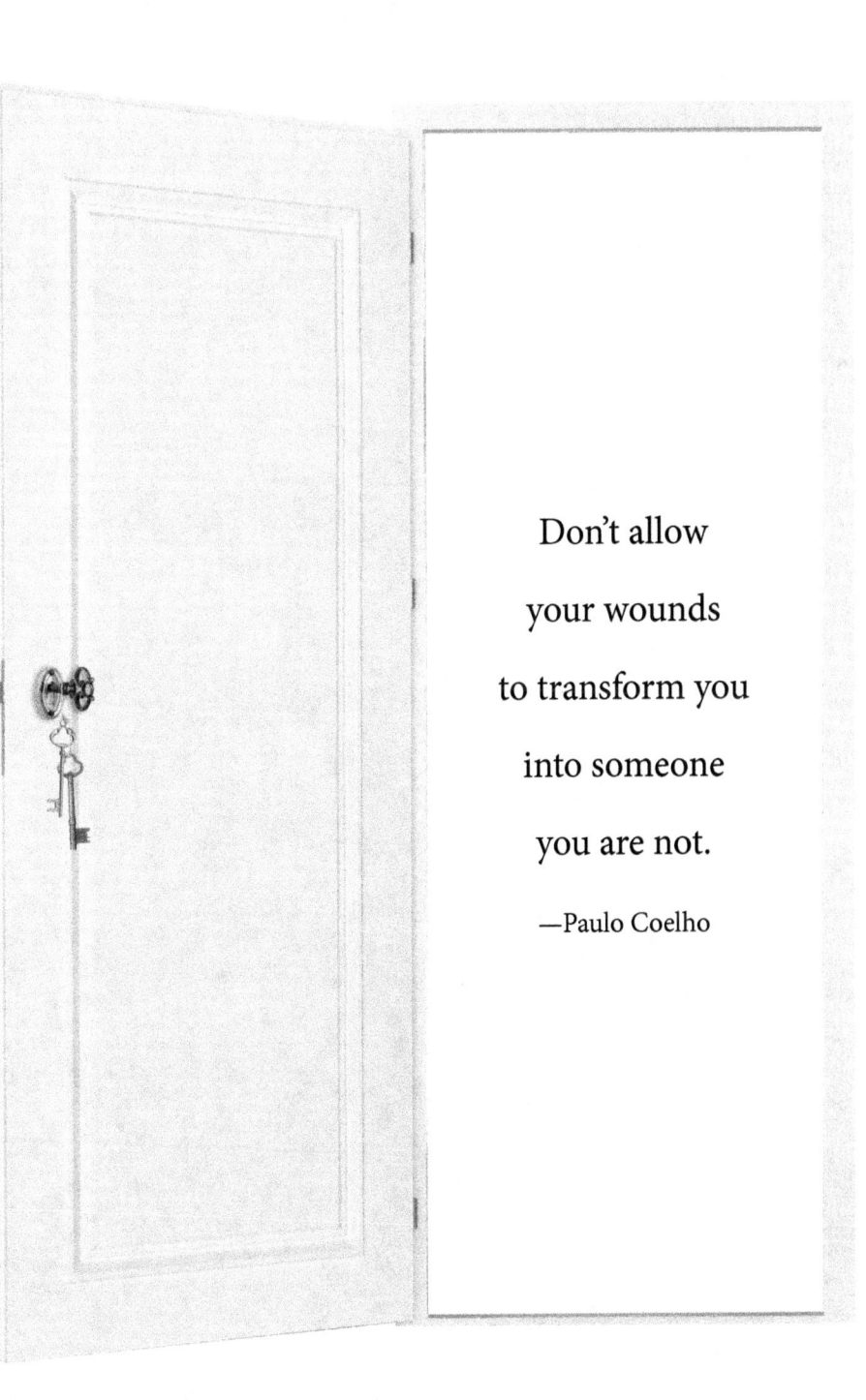

Don't allow your wounds to transform you into someone you are not.

—Paulo Coelho

CHAPTER THREE

How to Finance Your Home Purchase

Whether you decide to stay put after divorce or want to move on and get a fresh start, you need to know the financial ins and outs of securing a home loan. If you stay in the marital home, you need to refinance the present mortgage into your own name.

This chapter presents an overview of items required to make an informed decision about the right loan originator to work with and which loan program will be perfect for you. If you're moving to a new home, you can create a wish list of home features and a budget, then make sure they are compatible with each other.

Note: Check in your area for special loan options specific to your community.

Traditional Lending Sources

Several sources are available to provide you with a home mortgage, including:

- Mortgage Brokers
- Commercial Banks
- Financial Companies
- Federal Credit Unions
- Savings and Loan Associations

While one of these lenders may issue your mortgage, it is commonly insured by the U.S. federal government. To understand the difference between a conventional loan and a government-insured loan, visit **www.nolo.com/legal-encyclopedia/what-the-difference-between-conventional-fha-va-loan.html.**

Let's look at government loans first.

Federal Housing Authority

Your lender may provide you with a loan insured by the Federal Housing Association (FHA) but not originated by the FHA. You can use FHA loans to purchase or refinance your home. Know that an FHA loan must meet strict requirements such as loan limits based on the county and state in which the property is located as well as limits on the borrower's debt-to-income ratio.

Currently, FHA loans carry an Up Front Mortgage Insurance Premium (UFMIP), which is 1.75% of the loan amount. This has been recently reduced from 2.25% to make this loan more attractive. The monthly Mortgage Insurance Premium (MIP) can be variable, so check with your local loan originator for the exact figure. The FHA minimum down payment remains at 3.5% as of January 2016.

For more information about FHA loans, visit **www.fha.com.**

Reverse Mortgages

If you have equity in your home and are at least 62 years old, you can consider doing a reverse mortgage. It's an option if you'd benefit from additional income to pay off your mortgage, supplement your income, or pay for healthcare expenses. A reverse mortgage allows you to convert part of the equity in your home into cash without having to sell your home or pay additional monthly bills. Visit this website for more information: **https://www.consumer.ftc.gov/articles/0192-reverse-mortgages.**

Because a reverse mortgage can be complicated, take your time and do a thorough investigation. Work with a loan originator who specializes in this product, is patient, and has great communication skills.

Word to the Wise: The fees on a reverse mortgage are the same as a traditional FHA mortgage but are higher than a conventional mortgage because of the insurance cost. The largest costs are:
- FHA mortgage insurance
- Origination fee

Other considerations:
- The loan balance gets larger over time and the value of the estate/inheritance may decrease over time.
- Although Social Security and Medicare won't change, Medicaid and other needs-based government assistance can be affected if too much funding is withdrawn (and not spent) in one month.
- Many people find this program a bit more complex. It's key to consult with independent reverse mortgage counselors who specialize in this program.

Veterans Administration Programs

Qualifying members of the military, both active and retired, may be able to qualify for loans guaranteed by the Veterans Administration (VA). Similar to the Federal Housing Authority (FHA), the VA does not grant the loan; rather, it insures the loan for borrowers who meet the qualifications.

For more information, visit: **http://www.benefits.va.gov/homeloans/.**

Fannie Mae and Freddie Mac Programs

To help put home ownership within reach of the greatest number of Americans, U.S. Congress formed two institutional loan underwriters known as Fannie Mae, created in 1938, and Freddie Mac, created in 1970. These programs buy residential mortgages and mortgage-related securities from other lenders to help increase the supply of money for home loans.

Fannie Mae

Federal National Mortgage Association—plays a leading role in the mortgage ecosystem. By buying loans that banks and other lenders originate, it provides reliable, affordable mortgage financing in all markets. In turn, this enables the lending institutions to fund new loans and gives more people the opportunity to purchase or refinance homes.

In 2016, Fannie Mae and housing finance continue to evolve at a rapid pace. Although Fannie Mae is in conservatorship, it's considered to be a vastly different and stronger company than only a few years ago. Its conservators are the Treasury and the Federal Reserve, organizations that work to restore balance by conserving Fannie Mae's assets while supporting the mortgage market.

For more information, visit: **www.fanniemae.com/portal/index.html**.

Freddie Mac

Federal Home Mortgage Corporation—is a public government-sponsored enterprise created in 1970 to expand the secondary market for mortgages in the United States.

Along with the Fannie Mae, Freddie Mac buys mortgages on the secondary market, pools them, and sells them to investors on the open market as mortgage-backed securities. This secondary mortgage market increases the supply of funds available for mortgage lending. To learn more, visit: *www.freddiemac.com*.

Both of these government-sponsored entities (GSE) are regulated by the U.S. Department of Housing and Urban Development (HUD).

Non-Government-Backed Loans

Today, a loan is available to fit just about everyone's needs. You can select from the following loan programs:

- **Conventional Loan:** These are loans that aren't insured or guaranteed by government agencies such as the Federal Housing Authority or Veterans Administration.
- **15-year Mortgage:** This 15-year loan allows you to completely pay off your mortgage in 15 years.
- **30-Year Mortgage:** This 30-year mortgage extends your payments over a 30-year period.
- **Fixed-Rate Loan:** A fixed-rate loan applies one specified interest rate throughout the life of the loan.
- **Adjustable Rate Mortgage (ARM**): By definition, an ARM loan has an interest rate that fluctuates. It will initially apply the prevailing interest rates to your monthly payment, and the interest rate will then increase or decrease as interest rates rise and fall. This loan usually specifies a minimum and maximum interest rate that may be applied to your loan. As the name suggests, it adjusts annually. These minimum and maximums are usually based on the prime interest rate.
- **Interest Only Loans:** To keep payments down, some consumers choose "interest only" loans. These loans allow them to make monthly mortgage payments based only on the interest portion of the loan.

Word to the Wise: Carefully investigate this option for a loan. You're making payments only on the interest portion of your mortgage; you're not paying down the principal. Should home values tumble, you could owe more on your mortgage than your home is worth in the marketplace.

Note: You can use child support and maintenance to qualify for a mortgage, although specific rules apply. New guidelines were implemented in 2014 to protect the consumer and rules vary by state so please consult with a local loan originator. Be sure you understand these rules if you intend to use maintenance and child support to qualify for a mortgage.

Just remember the 6/36 rule. This means you must provide a consecutive six-month history of child support and maintenance being received. At the time the loan application is made, you must also show written proof that at least three years remain on the final divorce court order for these payments.

Note: Remember, if you are still navigating your divorce and it has not reached final agreement, you cannot apply for a loan. A divorce is a legal proceeding and you must wait for the final outcome. A loan application is never accepted when the applicant is involved in any legal proceeding.

The Cost of Your Loan

Typically, a homebuyer will make a down payment between 3.5 and 20 percent of the new home's sale price and finance the balance through a mortgage. Borrowing money for this mortgage requires paying various settlement fees that may average two to three percent of the total amount of your home loan.

In 2015, Congress enacted new mortgage rules called TRID or Integrated Disclosure Rules. These rules were implemented to protect consumers and ensure full disclosure of all loan fees. Specific fees charged may vary, but they typically include:

- Loan origination fee
- Closing fee
- Discount points
- Title insurance for the lender
- Document preparation fees
- Appraisal fees
- Recording fees

For more information, visit: **http://www.consumerfinance.gov/know-before-you-owe/.** (You'll also find these listed in Resources at the back of this book.)

Interest Rate vs. Annual Percentage Rate (APR)

Consumers often use the terms "APR" and "interest rate" interchangeably, but they are two very different charges. Be sure you know the difference when comparing lenders.

- The *interest rate* is the rate applied to your loan. Over the past few years, we have seen record low interest rates for mortgages, dipping to 2.75 percent.

- In contrast, the *APR or annual percentage rate* is the total annual cost for your loan. It will include the interest plus the fees to take out the loan. Be sure to ask lenders what their interest rate is as well as what the APR will be.

Note: Please beware that a loan originator might advertise an enticingly low interest rate but tack on exorbitantly high fees. This could make a loan program with a lower interest rate more expensive than a program that offers a higher interest rate but lower fees. It's imperative to compare your payment amounts over the life of the loan.

Note: The APR provides a more complete picture of loan costs than strictly the interest rate. Therefore, APR should be used to compare any loan programs you're considering.

Choosing a Loan Originator

All brokers must be registered with the Nationwide Mortgage Licensing System and Registry (NMLS). This is a national tracking system established by the Federal Secure and Fair Enforcement (SAFE) Mortgaging Act of 2008.

Your lender will give you several disclosure forms, so check on local requirements in your state. In general, make sure your prospective lender has had a good track record over the past few years. Check with your local Better Business Bureau to see if other consumers have lodged complaints against a lender. Ask for referrals from your Realtor® as well as friends, family members, and colleagues who might recommend a lender. Finally, watch for these warning signs:

- Higher than normal rates, excessive fees, and costly extras
- High-pressure sales tactics
- Pressure to buy add-ons such as pre-paid credit life insurance
- Excessive pre-payment penalties
- Over promising on when the loan will be funded

Strategies to Refinance Your Existing Home

Today, you can find as many ways to finance the purchase or refinance of your home as there are homebuyers. That's why it's vital to work with a loan originator who listens to your needs and can provide loan selections that are best for your personal situation.

Refinance the Home

Contrary to what some individuals believe, you cannot simply remove anyone's name from a deed. You can have the person who leaves sign over his or her ownership of the home to the other party with a Quit Claim Deed.

Note: Unless the present loan is assumable, a borrower's name can never be removed from a mortgage. A new mortgage must be taken out in the remaining person's name only. That means you'll have to remove your spouse's name from the mortgage and deed and qualify solely in your name. This solution works best if you have an independent income source and good credit.

Do an Equity Buyout

If you have enough equity in the home, you may also be able to finance enough of the home's value to provide your soon-to-be former spouse with a settlement for his or her share of the equity. Discuss this equity buyout option with your loan originator and legal advisor.

Assume the Existing Loan

In today's market, you likely can't assume an existing loan. A loan assumption allows the loan originator to change the current note and deed of trust to remove the seller's name and substitute the buyer's name. It requires the person assuming the loan to go through the complete qualifying process.

With good credit and your own income, it might be a simple matter to assume the existing loan. However, this strategy won't work if you need to provide your former spouse with a buyout sum and don't have the funds to do that. In this case, you might combine a loan assumption with another strategy such as a second mortgage or an equity line of credit for buyout funds.

100 Percent Loan

If you have good credit and a history of stable income, you may be able to finance 100 percent of the value of the home you want to purchase or refinance. This is called an 80/20 loan program. That means after taking out a first mortgage for 80 percent of the home's value, you simultaneously take out a second mortgage for the remaining 20 percent. Because the first mortgage is for only 80 percent of the home's value, no mortgage insurance is needed. The 2 to 3 percent cost of the loan could also be rolled into the loan, so you'd actually finance 102 to 103 percent.

Note: Mortgage insurance is required if the loan-to-value ratio or LTV is higher than 80 percent.

Word to the Wise: Approach this option carefully. If home values decline, you could owe more on the property than it is worth.

Home Equity Line of Credit (HELOC)

A program similar to getting a second mortgage is the equity line of credit. Like a second mortgage, you can use it to withdraw equity and pay off the party who is leaving the home.

To qualify for a HELOC, you'll need a good credit history, sufficient income, and enough equity in the home to secure the loan. Usually, the terms available with a home equity line of credit aren't as favorable as with a first or second mortgage.

Note: Equity lines of credit typically have variable interest rates that rise and fall with market conditions. While HELOC interest rates tend to be lower than most credit card interest rates, they are often more expensive than first or second mortgages.

Interest Only Loans

To keep payments low, some consumers choose interest only loans that permit them to make monthly mortgage payments based only on the interest portion of the loan. The term of the loan can be 5, 10, or even 15 years.

Because payments cover only the interest and not the principal (the actual amount of the loan), keep in mind you're counting on market values to appreciate. Should real estate values decrease (as with the 100 percent loan), you could be placed in the financially compromised position of owing more on your home than it's worth.

Creating Your Own Solution

The loan program that works best varies based on personal circumstances. It could be one of the solutions discussed in this chapter or something else entirely. Explore your options by having a frank conversation with your Realtor®, loan originator, and financial advisor about the pros and cons for you.

Note: Use the financial tools in Chapter Five of this book. There, you'll find a long list of tools that will be essential as you move through the home buying process.

For support with mortgage questions or concerns, contact the Consumer Financial Protection Bureau. Call 855-411-2372 or visit: **http://www.consumerfinance.gov/**.

What Lenders Need From Buyers

You can expedite the time spent completing an online application if you have gathered the following documents for the loan originator.

General
- Social Security numbers
- Divorce papers
- Green cards for resident aliens
- Employment verifications

- Two most recent paycheck stubs
- Tax returns for the last two years
- Three most recent bank statements

Assets

- Savings accounts (balances, account numbers, and institutions)
- Credit union (balances, account numbers, and institutions)
- Mutual funds (balances, account numbers, and institutions)
- IRAs or 401(k)s (balances, account numbers, and institutions)
- Equity in current home
- Cash flows from rental properties
- Pensions or annuities
- Maintenance and child support payments received
- Life insurance—the face amount and cash value

Debts

- Mortgage and home equity loans
- Monthly bills
- Credit card balances
- Student loans
- Car loans
- Maintenance and child support payments

Note: If you are self-employed, you must also provide balance sheets and company tax returns.

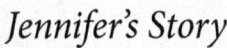

Jennifer's Story

When Jennifer and her husband of 15 years decided to part ways, she knew immediately that, for her kids' sake, she needed to stay put. Her daughter, a social butterfly in her senior year of high school, would have found a move to a new home and new school highly disruptive. Jennifer's middle school son was involved in sports and adamantly stated he, too, wanted to stay in their present home. So even though the home wasn't Jennifer's ideal, she agreed to wait before relocating.

Yet she wasn't idle while waiting for her kids to get older. She engaged a loan originator to confirm she would qualify for a mortgage and got clear on her housing budget. She started shopping online to acquaint herself with the local market and began working with her Realtor® to identify elements of her new "dream house." With no pressure to move, Jennifer had the luxury of time to carefully look through a wide range of properties. She wanted to be sure she'd buy the right new home for her and her family.

This process took Jennifer 18 months, but she finally found her dream home in the ideal location so this energetic, socially active woman could be close to friends and the arts.

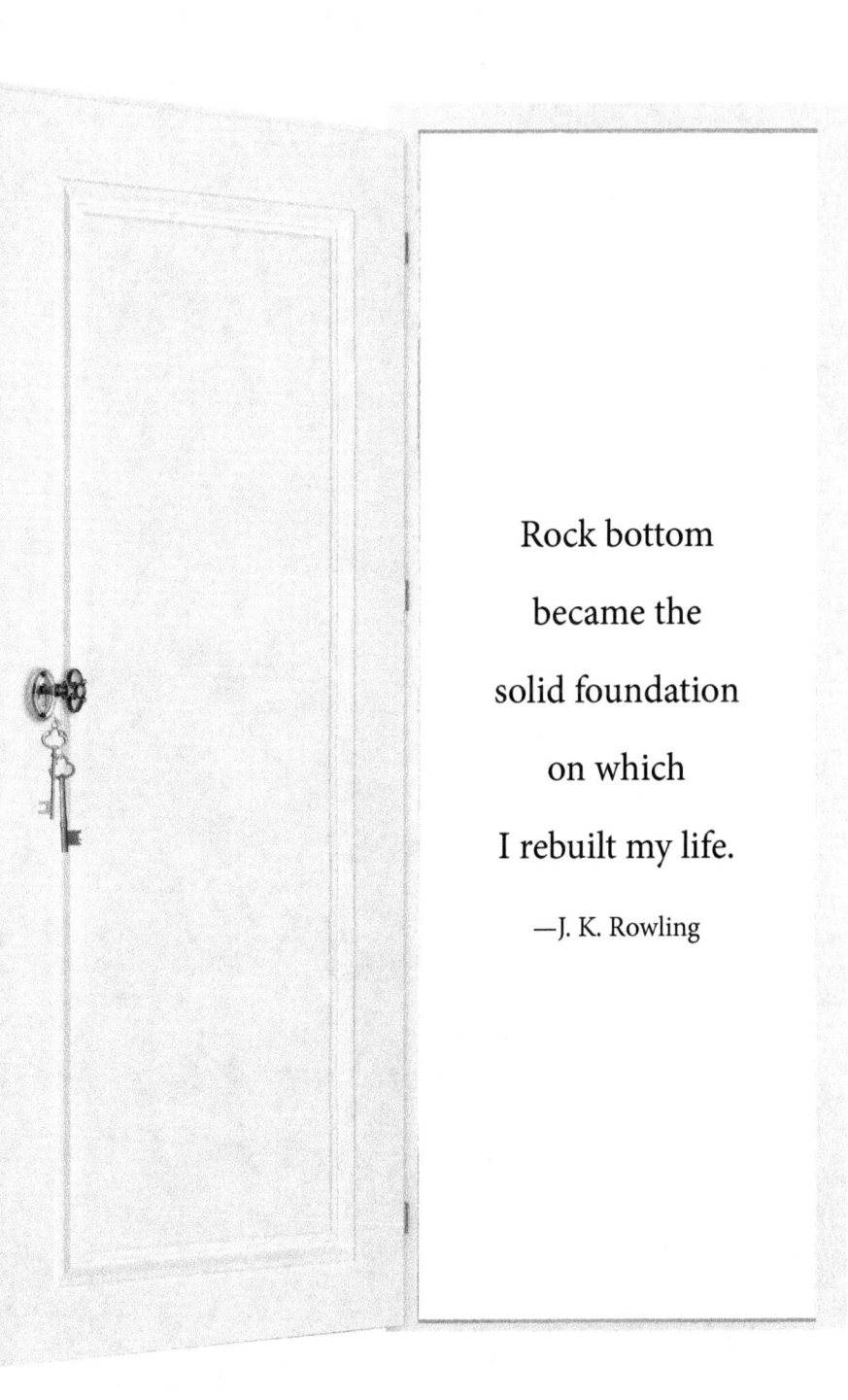

Rock bottom became the solid foundation on which I rebuilt my life.

—J. K. Rowling

CHAPTER FOUR

The Real Estate Buy/Sell Process

This chapter provides guidelines for selling and purchasing a home. Because the real estate process varies from state to state, check with your Realtor® for guidelines in your area.

Selling Your Home

You've considered the option to keep the marital home but have decided to sell. What does that involve?

The Realtor® you work with to sell your house will often be the one who helps you find a new place to call home. Having the same person for both buying and selling provides continuity, and here's the bonus. Often Realtors® reduce their commission on a sale if they can help that person purchase a new home.

Also interview a number of brokers and compare their marketing programs. Having a strong knowledge of cutting-edge technology is important as well as a powerful Internet presentation of your home. Currently, 97 percent of buyers are shopping online, not only locally but internationally.

To connect with the right Realtor®, ask friends, family, co-workers, and divorce team members for referrals. Your working relationship must be comfortable because you'll be working closely over an extended time and sharing a lot of personal information.

Home Selling Checklist

Choose the Realtor® whom you trust to sell your home for the highest price in the least amount of time. Be sure to ask for their estimated timeline and a list of steps they will take in the selling process. A list may include the following:

- Review comparables and establish a sales price.
- Review and sign documents, complete all disclosures.
- Organize, repurpose, make cosmetic improvements, and stage the home.
- Take professional photos and perhaps produce a video with 3D videos.
- Enter the home into the local MLS or Information Exchange and national Real Estate Information websites.
- Set up an automatic email to monitor neighborhood competition—new listings, under contract, or sold homes.
- Contact the showing service company to schedule showings.
- Place a lock box on the home to indicate entry.
- Schedule showings according to the owner's requests.
- Send feedback requests to all showing agents.
- Notify owner via email of all known feedback.
- Make adjustments (e.g., pricing, condition of the home) based on feedback.
- Receive an offer and begin negotiations.

Note: Suppose the offer you are considering is contingent on the sale of the buyer's home. Make a counter proposal that says you will accept that offer once you review the offer on the buyer's home. This includes a conversation with that buyer's lender to

confirm qualification and the timeframe of contract dates being met. Your Realtor® will guide you through this process.
- Order the title commitment.
- Schedule inspections.
- Review inspection objections and negotiate resolutions, assisting with bids as needed.
- Schedule appraisal and confirm your Realtor® will meet the appraiser with an Appraisal Package.
- Keep communication open with the buyer's loan originator.
- Schedule a closing date.
- Review closing documents with the seller 24 hours prior to the closing date.

The selling process is further fleshed out in the buying process, which is discussed next.

Make Your New Home a Reality

Now the fun begins! Your home is under contract or sold, and you have the financial piece and budget confirmed. Now it's time to make a wish list of priorities for your new home. There will always be compromises made, but it's helpful to have a starting point.

Making this wish list will not only clarify things for you, it will also aid your real estate professional in expediting the search. Consider these factors:

- **Where do you want to live?** Are your kids still in school? If so, how important is it for them to remain in their current schools?
- **If you work** or have to drop kids at daycare, what's a reasonable commute time? Have you test-driven the commute from the neighborhoods you are considering?

- **What does your lifestyle look like?** Do you enjoy cultural activities such as opera, ballet, symphony, or theater? Is the outdoors more your style where you can hike, bike, or run? Finding a home close to the activities you like is important.
- **Where is your social network?** Do you want to be close to family and friends? How close?
- **Can you afford the homes that fit your needs** in your targeted neighborhood? Would you compromise on certain items on your wish list to live in certain neighborhoods?
- **Do you have specific furniture** you must accommodate? (e.g., a baby grand piano?)
- **If you have young children,** is this potentially a neighborhood where your children can find playmates?
- **What features do you want in a home?** How many bedrooms and bathrooms? Do you need a garage and home office?
- **Do you have health requirements** that limit your ability to climb stairs? Is a one-story home essential? What other specifics need to be reflected in your home?
- **What is the prospective neighborhood like during various** times of day or in the evening?

Finding a House On Your Own

Currently, 97 percent of homebuyers are shopping online. You can certainly spend hours taking virtual tours, or you can drive desirable neighborhoods and visit every open house on the market. If this is your only search strategy, it may take weeks or months to identify an acceptable home. In a rapidly moving market where properties sell quickly, you could miss out on a lot of opportunities.

Remember that as a buyer, traditionally you won't be expected to pay your real estate professional. The seller compensates the listing broker and that fee is customarily split with the buyer's broker. Therefore, you have no financial incentive *not* to use a real estate professional to guide you in this complicated transaction. And you can benefit from the many advantages.

For Sale By Owners (FSBOs)

To save paying a sales commission, some sellers try to market their homes by themselves. These are called For Sale By Owners or FSBOs. Unfortunately, these sellers usually don't discount their asking price accordingly. They should deduct the selling price by the amount of commission they will *not* have to pay to the real estate agent. Why? By doing this, the final net equity to sellers will equal that of comparable homes when the seller *did* pay a commission.

Statistics show that in most "For Sale By Owners" (FSBOs) situations, the owners are eventually willing to pay the buyer's broker commission, or they ultimately list their home with a real estate agent.

Real estate has become an increasingly complex and litigious business. Without a Realtor® by your side, you'll miss out on having valuable expertise to steer clear of home-buying pitfalls, and you may even ultimately pay more for your new home. Plus working with an experienced Realtor® will simplify your life. This professional will consider your wish list, evaluate available properties, and show you homes that most closely align with your needs and budget. With knowledge of the current real estate tools, your Realtor® can suggest online resources to expedite your search. An example would be setting up an automatic email system to notify you of new listings the moment they enter your local market.

Most important, your Realtor® knows the ins and outs of the entire process. S/he can guide you through your search and purchase, making these steps as enjoyable and stress-free as possible.

Public Home Search Websites

Shopping for a home online is easier than ever due to a number of information exchanges available to consumers. Be aware that the information these public exchanges provide is generally not as accurate or up-to-date as your Realtor®'s local access to information.

The top public information exchanges for home searches:
- *Realtor.com®*
- *Experian.com*
- *Zillow.com*
- *Trulia.com*
- *Yahoo.com*

Find the Right Realtor®

The Realtor® who helps you buy or sell a home plays a crucial role during this phase of your life. It makes sense to choose someone with whom you feel completely comfortable. You'll be sharing many personal details such as your financial profile, your family history, and your personal preferences.

Real Estate Agent Versus Realtor®

Most states regulate the real estate profession through a licensing process. This process requires real estate agents to successfully complete a course of study and pass a rigorous exam. This is then followed by a thorough background check and finger printing. Anyone who successfully completes these steps can lawfully practice real estate sales as a Realtor®, a sales agent, or a broker. *However, there is an important distinction.*

Realtors® are not only licensed by the state in which they practice, but they must also successfully complete a course in ethics administered by the National Association of Realtors® (NAR). In addition, Realtors® must adhere to a code of ethics for professional practices and maintain their membership in good standing with a local board of Realtors® in order to use the Realtor® registered designation. There are licensed agents practicing real estate without affiliating with NAR.

You can find a Realtor® by asking friends, family members, or colleagues for a referral and holding interviews with two or three prospective candidates. You're best to limit your search to full-time professionals who are fully committed to their profession and to meeting your goals.

Following your interviews, evaluate a prospective Realtor® using these criteria:

- How well does the Realtor® know the community you're considering?
- How long has the Realtor® been in business?
- What is the prospective Realtor's® professional demeanor? Does s/he inspire confidence? Will s/he be able to work effectively on your behalf with potential buyers, sellers, and their Realtors®? Remember, your Realtor® acts as your messenger since buyers and sellers are rarely in direct communication.
- How well do you connect with this person? Does s/he listen and understand your needs? Spending hours visiting homes that don't remotely interest you can be frustrating and a total waste of time—a scenario that occurs when your Realtor® hasn't understood your needs and goals.
- What professional designations does s/he hold?

Word to the Wise: The Realtor® you choose should be sensitive to your needs and help ensure your goals are met. If that person fails to respond to your concerns, it might be time to make a change.

Professional Credentials

When a Realtor® continues his/her professional education to obtain advanced designations, it can be considered tangible proof s/he cares about the profession and wants to provide the highest level of service. You may encounter these advanced designations:

- **GRI:** Graduate of Real Estate Institute. Achieved by those who are successful graduates of the Real Estate Institutes' advanced courses.
- **CRS:** Awarded by the Council of Residential Specialists to only four percent of Realtors®, this designation is based on certain production requirements and the professional's participation in advanced classes.
- **CREDS:** Certified Real Estate Divorce Specialist
- **CLHMS:** Certified Luxury Home Marketing Specialist
- **MRE:** Masters in Real Estate
- **ABR:** Accredited Buyer Representative
- **SRES:** Senior Real Estate Specialist

Agency Representation vs. Transaction Broker

Most people choose to work with a Realtor® who provides them with agency representation. This means the professional works as your advocate; you have a fiduciary bond and your best interests are represented. By a wide margin, most consumers choose to have a Realtor® represent them as either a buyer's or seller's agent.

A few consumers choose a different path, though, and contract with a Realtor® to act as a transaction broker. In contrast to an agent who acts as an advocate during the transaction, a transaction broker is a neutral party who facilitates the transaction. Brokers have no loyalty to either party. However, like Realtors®, they are required to perform their duties honestly, ethically, and fairly.

Note: The terminology may vary from state to state, so please check on procedures in the state you will be doing business.

Pre-Qualified vs. Pre-Approved

Before you begin looking at prospective homes, work with a reputable loan originator to get pre-qualified or pre-approved for a home loan. Ask your Realtor® or other members of your divorce team for referrals to loan originators they've worked with.

While it's essential you check with a loan originator for a *pre-qualification* to buy before you begin visiting homes, take this process one step further and get a *pre-approval* for your home loan. This is key to identifying you as a strong buyer in the eyes of the seller and can be an advantage in price negotiations.

With a *pre-qualification,* a loan originator takes a cursory look at your financial picture and, based on the information you provide, assesses your likely ability to qualify for a certain loan amount. That's all that is needed for a pre-qualification.

With a *pre-approval,* you receive a conditional commitment from the lender to provide you with a specific loan package. That package is based on your credit report and financial picture as provided on your application. This indicates the verification process has been started, usually with an underwriting program. Being pre-approved is a winning strategy and especially important when the market is competitive.

Once your file has been completed, it passes to the underwriter who reviews all the documents and verifies the information. Full loan approval is subject to conditions such as a satisfactory appraisal of the home, a title review, and assurance your financial circumstances don't change between the time of the pre-approval and loan closing. Be sure you don't make changes to your credit situation since a credit report will be run again prior to closing. If you make a major purchase such as buying a car at this late stage, you face a strong chance your loan will be denied.

Locking in your loan terms helps ensure you receive the specific terms discussed with your loan originator. It verifies your interest rate, loan origination fees, and settlement costs. Written documentation of your interest rate is a must to guarantee that rate for 30 to 45 days. Extending terms beyond this timeframe usually requires a fee.

Interest rates fluctuate and affect how much home you can afford, so it's critical to lock in the terms of your loan. A diligent loan originator will watch interest rates and provide notice when it's considered advantageous for you to lock in your interest rate. To expedite the process for all parties, complete the financial worksheets in Chapter Five and gather the documents itemized in that chapter to share with your loan originator.

Let's say you have found your dream home—finally! You've looked at several properties, obtained your loan pre-approval, and found the home that fits your needs and your budget. Next, we'll look at various parts of the process, which can vary by state.

Offer to Purchase Process

Your Realtor® drafts an offer to purchase, officially called a Contract to Buy and Sell Real Estate. The price you offer depends on the condition of the home, comparable sales, and current local market activity. If it's a seller's market and others show interest in the house you want, you may be required to offer more than the listed sales price to edge out the competition. On the other hand, in a slow market, you may be able to offer less than the asking price. Your Realtor® can provide specific information and guide you to formulate a winning strategy.

Consider these questions before you and your Realtor® submit your contract to the seller:

- What is your offered price for the home including how much earnest money you'll put down, what type of loan you are using, and whether you have a pre-approval letter?
- Is your offer contingent on the sale of your existing home?
- Is the proposed closing date and possession day compatible with the seller's needs?
- What financial arrangements are needed (e.g., having the seller contribute to closing costs)?
- Will the seller provide a home warranty?

Contract Contingencies

Contingencies built into your offer usually include requirements that the home successfully passes professional inspections and that a professional appraiser, hired by the lender, values the home at or above the sales price. Additional contingencies include being able to secure financing to purchase the home and ensuring the title is clear. (More about these items later in this chapter.)

When the contract is submitted to the seller, the buyer submits a sum called earnest money to the seller to show the buyer is making the offer in good faith. The earnest money is held by a third party in a trust account and will be credited to the buyer at closing. If the seller doesn't accept your terms or the sale falls through because a contingency isn't met, your earnest money will be returned to you.

After your Realtor® presents your offer to the seller's agent, it will be either accepted or rejected, or it will initiate a counter offer from the seller. If you receive a counter offer, you can accept, reject, or counter that offer with one of your own. Negotiations could continue for a time before you and the seller come to agreeable terms.

Note: In a competitive market, the seller may be reviewing additional offers. Your Realtor® can help you submit a compelling offer. For example, writing a personal letter to the seller about a strong desire to own this home can be effective.

Lock-in Loan Terms

If your offer is accepted and you haven't been pre-approved by a lender for a specific loan package, now is the time to lock in your mortgage interest rate and the particulars of the loan financing. (See Chapter Three for a refresher on the elements of mortgages, including what expenses lenders may charge.) Keep in mind that you have nothing to lose and everything to gain by securing pre-approval and locking in your loan terms ahead of time. Rising interest rates can lower the value of the home you can afford, so locking in the rate before even viewing the house provides assurance you can finance the one you have your eye on.

You might find buying a home exciting, but it's also stressful. You can reduce the stress around qualifying for a loan by securing your financing first. It's a major key to your success!

Title Search and Title Insurance

Another critical step in the home-buying process is the title search, conducted by a title company. The title search verifies the seller has clear title to the property and the legal right to sell.

What Does "Title" Mean to You as a Buyer?

"Title" is a term to describe legal rights to own, control, or sell a property. It can also describe the rights to use the property you're considering purchasing. Because you want protection from future title issues, gather all the information you can about the property for a title search and then assess the best title insurance coverage to purchase. A reputable title company completes both of these tasks for you and can be designated by either buyer or seller.

Be sure to ask your Realtor® to confirm that the title company is in good standing and has a track record in your community. Get assurance that the title company will be available to you in the future if a problem arises with the title.

Word to the Wise: Unfortunately, over recent years, many title companies have gone out of business, so it's important to select carefully.

Title Search and Commitment

Specifically, the designated title company researches county records for any information about the specified address. This information is then disclosed on a title commitment for your review. In reading through the title commitment, you might note liens against the property such as an outstanding mortgage or tax bill. You might also find restrictive covenants or agreements affecting the use of the property. Some examples would be an easement for utilities, permission for others to use or cross through the property, or mineral and water rights held by another entity. For concerns about items noted in the title commitment, it's best to seek legal advice to resolve these matters before you move forward with your purchase.

Because having a clear title to your new home is imperative, purchasing title insurance is necessary. This valuable coverage gives you financial protection in the event the title search did not identify existing problems with the title. Common problems with a property's title can include tax liens, judgments, easements, or mistakes in the public record. Should any of these problems go unidentified until after your sale has been completed, your owner's title insurance policy protects you by paying any claims or legal fees arising in your defense of the title.

The cost for title insurance can be paid by either buyer or seller. The buyer is also required to provide a title policy for the mortgage company to protect the investor's interests. This charge is a line item on the disclosure of loan costs to the buyer.

Note: If anyone has placed a lien against the home, that party can stop the sale from going forward until the lien is removed. In all cases, the seller will have to pay off any liens before the sale proceeds.

Home Inspection

Your offer to the seller should be contingent on a home inspection—an essential step that confirms the home is in good, safe condition with all systems and appliances functioning. As a new home owner, naturally you want to avoid any immediate repair surprises after you move in.

Don't be concerned if the home inspector comes up with a list of items that need attention. Inspections almost always find problems to be addressed. The good news is that most issues can be readily resolved.

Among the elements the home inspector evaluates are:

- Workability of the electrical, mechanical, plumbing, heating, and other systems
- Presence of radon gas and if so, determine if it's within acceptable limits of 4.0 picocuries as established by the EPA

- Condition of the roof, ceiling, walls, basement, and exterior
- Presence of mold in the house
- Functioning of septic tanks, wells, and sewer lines
- Presence of termites or past termite damage
- Workability of the appliances provided

A selection of home inspections is available and includes:
- General inspection
- Radon gas inspection
- Well test (includes pump and flow rate, capacity, and recovery rate)
- Well potability (is the water safe for consumption?)
- Septic system inspection
- Sewer line scope inspection
- Mold and/or mildew inspection
- Methamphetamine inspection
- Lead-based paint inspection
- Termite inspection
- Chimneys inspection
- Thermography (to detect hidden areas of heat loss, air infiltration, or moisture intrusion) inspection

Top 10 Most Common Inspection Issues

1. Basement or crawl space is damp or wet.

2. Plumbing is defective; fixtures leak.

3. Furnace requires cleaning, adjustments, or certification.

4. Electrical or wiring is unsafe.

5. Roof issues require repairs or a full replacement.

6. Exterior grading shows problems.

7. Foundation or concrete shows signs of movement due to settling or deterioration.

8. Windows and doors do not operate correctly.

9. Wood surfaces including decks, window trim, or siding show signs of rot.

10. Mildew, radon, or lead-based paint is present.

With the completed inspection report in hand, you have important information to guide you as you proceed with your purchase and negotiations. If the report indicates a need for substantial repairs, you can request the seller complete them prior to closing. Alternatively, you can negotiate a new purchase price or receive a credit at closing.

Note: If the news about the home's condition is unacceptable and you can't reach a resolution with the seller, you can terminate the transaction provided you act within your inspection objection deadlines.

Word to the Wise: It's always advisable for the party buying the marital home to have a professional inspection done. No matter how long you have lived in the home or believe everything is operational, an inspection can point out potential pitfalls. The inspection results are also a factor in determining the buyout or purchase price.

Appraisal Process

As you move forward with your mortgage financing, your lender will require assurance that the home is worth the price you're paying. To achieve that, the lender engages a licensed appraiser to appraise the property. The appraiser looks at all the features of the home and compares it with other homes nearby to determine if the home's fair market value is equal to the contract price. The result of the appraisal is crucial in setting the price.

There's no down side if the appraisal comes in higher than the contract price, but if the appraiser finds the home is worth less than you're paying, it can stop the transaction from moving forward. At this point, you have these three options:

- Make up the difference between the appraisal and contract price with cash out of your pocket,
- Go back to the seller and attempt to renegotiate the purchase price, or
- Walk away from the home.

Home Warranty

One of the joys of home ownership is maintaining your home, knowing there will always be items needing attention and repair. It's been estimated that 1% of the value of the property should be budgeted annually for repairs and maintenance. That means, for example, if the home is valued at $300,000, then you would budget $3,000 annually for repairs and maintenance.

When dealing with repairs, would you appreciate being able to call someone who would send a service technician, especially when you'd only have to pay for the service call or receive a reduced rate? Purchasing a Home Warranty through a reputable company can provide this service and peace of mind while eliminating the question of where to turn. These programs are available to sellers and may be considered an incentive to buyers. They're also available for buyers to purchase directly from the warranty company.

Here's how a Home Warranty works. The homeowner and home warranty company sign a contract agreeing to provide discounted repair and replacement of major home components such as air conditioning, furnace, electrical system, and major appliances (dryers, washers, and refrigerators). While all warranty plans provide some coverage, increased coverage for optional components might also be available for an additional charge.

The home warranty company has an agreement with approved service providers, so whenever something covered by the warranty breaks down, the homeowner just has to call the home warranty company. A representative in turn sends a service provider to diagnose the problem. If the warranty covers the repair or replacement, the technician completes the work. The homeowner pays only a small service fee. If the problem requires an additional tradesman such as a plumber or electrician, the homeowner pays the service fee for both.

Home warranties, which cost a few hundred dollars, can be paid upfront or through a payment plan. The plans vary between basic and extended policies, depending on the property type. Some policies include coverage for the garage while others do not, so be sure to check.

Home warranty owners are not necessarily free from spending any money on home repairs. They have to pay for repairs or problems not covered by the warranty company if they didn't buy coverage for the item needing repair. If the company denies a claim due to poor maintenance, the homeowner has to pay the service fee and also repair costs.

Review the options and ratings of companies that provide warranties in your area and ask your Realtor® for recommendations. For a list of Home Warranty companies, visit: **https://www.consumersadvocate.org/home-warranties/best-home-warranties.**

Title Transfer

The process by which real estate transactions are finalized varies by state. In some states, all the required funds are held in an escrow account until the parties sign the paperwork and officially close the sale. This is frequently done in two parts, and the buyer and seller never meet.

In other states, both parties bring funds or wire them to a closing meeting. The title company or a designated third party prepares the documents, collects and disburses all funds, and pays off any liens against the property. The final documents are signed, and the deed is delivered to the buyer and then recorded. The seller receives a check for the equity in the home. The title now passes to the new owner.

After this process is completed, the buyers receive the keys to their new home. They're free to move in on the agreed-upon possession date. Congratulations!

Joel and Brenda's Story

Brenda had been the primary breadwinner in her marriage to Joel. Because they're divorcing, Joel was concerned that his standard of living would plummet. He needed guidance to land on his feet financially without saddling Brenda with huge settlement demands.

To create a strategy regarding the marital home, Joel and Brenda's Realtor® looked at their present home to establish fair market value and equity. Then a loan originator reviewed their separate incomes and credit information to confirm their ability to either keep the marital home or purchase a new one. It was decided Brenda would stay in the home and give Joel a buyout settlement. He would use this equity amount for a down payment, which helped him qualify for a loan in his own name.

Joel wanted a new home that was compatible with his needs both financially and personally and also provided a comfortable space for their children. After the divorce, Brenda and the children remained in their home while Joel began his new life in a place suited to his new life style and financial circumstances.

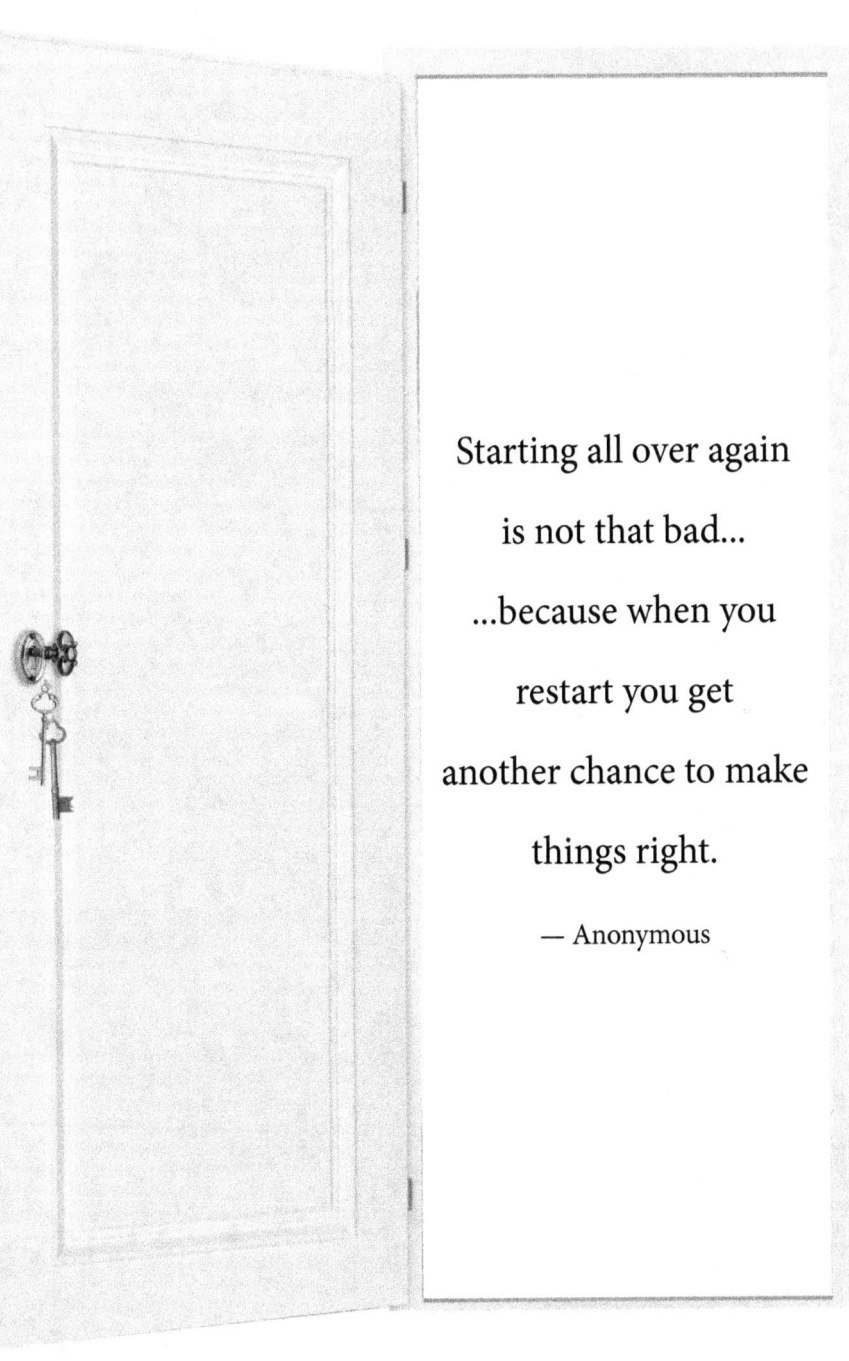

Starting all over again is not that bad... ...because when you restart you get another chance to make things right.

— Anonymous

CHAPTER FIVE

Your Personal Workbook

In this section, you will find lots of useful tools to help you gather the essential information you'll need in the home buying process. The financial information worksheets will serve as a valuable resource to assist your lender in assessing your borrowing potential.

Financial Overview
Vital Statistics

Your name _____

Your Current Address _____

City _____

State _____ Zip _____

Daytime Phone _____

Evening Phone _____

Email _____

Social Security Number _____

Date of Birth _____

Marital Status: ☐ Single   ☐ Married   ☐ Divorced   ☐ Widowed

Income and Source

Salary and Wages _____

Investment Income and Dividends _____

Social Security _____

Pension or Retirement Plan _____

Other Income _____

_____

_____

Total Income _____

Family Budget
Monthly Income

Net Wages $ _____

Spousal Support $ _____

Child Support $ _____

Other Income $ _____

Total Income $ _____

Monthly Expenses
Auto

Auto Expenses (Fuel, Service) $ _____

Auto Loan $ _____

Total Auto $ _____

Child Rearing

Child Care $ _____

School Expenses $ _____

Education/Activities $ _____

College Savings $ _____

Total Child Rearing $ _____

Food

Groceries $ _____

Dining Out $ _____

Total Food $ _____

Utilities

Gas and Electric $ _____

Water and Sewer $ _____

Trash $ _____

TV and Cable $ _____

Phone $ _____

Total Utilities $ _____

Insurance

Auto Insurance $ _____

Disability Insurance $ _____

Hazard Insurance $ _____

Health Insurance $ _____

Life Insurance $ _____

Total Insurance $ _____

Housing Expenses

Mortgage, Rent or Lease Payment $ _____

Second Mortgage $ _____

Home Equity Loan $ _____

Property Taxes $ _____

Homeowners Association $ _____

Mortgage Insurance $ _____

Repair and Maintenance* $ _____

Rule of thumb, use 1% of home's value

Total Housing Expenses $ _____

Medical

Doctor $ _____

Dentist $ _____

Vision $ _____

Other $ _____

Total Medical $ _____

Credit and Installment Debt

Credit Cards $ _____

Other Debt $ _____

Total Debt $ _____

Personal Care

Clothing $ _____

Barber/Stylist $ _____

Laundry/Dry Cleaning $ _____

Total Personal Care $ _____

Miscellaneous

Professional Expenses $ _____

Entertainment and Recreation $ _____

Vacations $ _____

Gifts $ _____

Charitable Giving $ _____

Total Miscellaneous $ _____

Mortgage Calculator

To determine if you will qualify for a mortgage, you need to demonstrate to a lender that your debts—especially long-term debts—are in line with your income. Use the calculation worksheet below to see what your current debt to income ratio is, and how that compares to what lenders want to see in prospective borrowers.

Total monthly income	$_____
Total housing expenses	$_____
Housing expenses as a % of income:	%_____
Total long-term debt	$_____
Total housing expenses	$_____
Total Debt Service	$_____

Total Debt Service as a % of income: %_____

Employment History

Please provide your last two year's work history, starting with your most recent employment.

Employer's Name _____

Supervisor's Name _____

Address _____

_____

Phone _____

Start Date _____

End Date _____

Current / Ending Salary _____

Employer's Name _____

Supervisor's Name _____

Address _____

_____

Phone _____

Start Date _____

End Date _____

Current / Ending Salary _____

Employer's Name _____

Supervisor's Name _____

Address _____

_____

Phone _____

Start Date _____

End Date _____

Current / Ending Salary _____

Employer's Name _____

Supervisor's Name _____

Address _____

_____

Phone _____

Start Date _____

End Date _____

Current / Ending Salary _____

Employer's Name _____

Supervisor's Name _____

Address _____

_____

Phone _____

Start Date _____

End Date _____

Current / Ending Salary _____

Please explain any gaps in your work history:

_____

_____

_____

_____

_____

_____

_____

Moving Expenses Worksheet

Down Payment $_____
Down payments may range from zero down to an average of 20% of the home's current value. Of course, the more you put down, the smaller your mortgage.

Moving Expenses $_____
Include here the cost of packing and moving your personal belongings into your new home. Even if you plan to do it yourself, factor in the cost of boxes, packing materials, and renting a truck, if necessary.

Settlement Costs $_____
These are lender-required expenses such as document fees, transaction fees, etc. These expenses should be detailed in your Good Faith Estimate, and usually run about 2 to 3 percent of the total loan amount.

Settling-in Costs $_____
You may need to fix up your new home to suit your aesthetic tastes or lifestyle needs. Add those expenses here.

Closing Costs $_____
Usually amounting to 3 to 6 percent of the amount of your mortgage, these fees represent lender's fees. Depending on the terms you negotiate, the lender may waive these fees.

Cost of Selling Your Existing Home $_____
Before you can sell your home, you may need to make repairs and improvements to make it inspection ready.

Total Cost of Moving $_____

Liabilities
Mortgages

Your Primary Residence _____

Fair Market Value _____

Address _____

Owner _____

City _____

State _____ Zip _____

County _____

Mortgage Company _____

Address of Mortgage Company_____

Loan Number _____

Property Causality Insurance Company _____

Address _____

Home Owner's Policy Number_____

Auto Loans

Auto Make / Model / Year_____

Fair Market Value _____

If there is an associated loan, please provide:_____

Lender Name _____

Address _____

Loan Number _____

Current Balance _____

Monthly Payment_____

Auto Make / Model / Year _____

Fair Market Value _____

If there is an associated loan, please provide: _____

Lender Name _____

Address _____

Loan Number _____

Current Balance _____

Monthly Payment _____

Credit Cards
Please list all credit card, department store and other revolving charge accounts:

Name of Creditor _____

Account Number _____

Address _____

Phone _____

Current Balance _____

Monthly Payment _____

Date Opened _____

Name of Creditor _____

Account Number _____

Address _____

Phone _____

Current Balance _____

Monthly Payment _____

Date Opened _____

Name of Creditor _____

Account Number _____

Address _____

Phone _____

Current Balance _____

Monthly Payment _____

Date Opened _____

Name of Creditor _____

Account Number _____

Address _____

Phone _____

Current Balance _____

Monthly Payment _____

Date Opened _____

Name of Creditor _____

Account Number _____

Address _____

Phone _____

Current Balance _____

Monthly Payment _____

Date Opened _____

Name of Creditor _____

Account Number _____

Address _____

Phone _____

Current Balance _____

Monthly Payment _____

Date Opened _____

Student Loans

Name of Creditor _____

Account Number _____

Address _____

Phone _____

Current Balance _____

Monthly Payment _____

Date Opened _____

Name of Creditor _____

Account Number _____

Address _____

Phone _____

Current Balance _____

Monthly Payment _____

Date Opened _____

Name of Creditor _____

Account Number _____

Address _____

Phone _____

Current Balance _____

Monthly Payment _____

Date Opened _____

Other Debts

Name of Creditor _____

Account Number _____

Address _____

Phone _____

Current Balance _____

Monthly Payment _____

Date Opened _____

Name of Creditor _____

Account Number _____

Address _____

Phone _____

Current Balance _____

Monthly Payment _____

Date Opened _____

Name of Creditor _____

Account Number _____

Address _____

Phone _____

Current Balance _____

Monthly Payment _____

Date Opened _____

Assets

Bank Accounts
For each account, please attach a copy of your most recent statements.

Institution _____

Address _____

Type _____

Account # _____

Owner _____

Value _____

This account is a:_____

Please indicate the type of account:

☐ Checking ☐ Savings ☐ Certificates of Deposit ☐ Safety Deposit Box

Institution _____

Address _____

Type _____

Account # _____

Owner _____

Value _____

This account is a:_____

Please indicate the type of account:

☐ Checking ☐ Savings ☐ Certificates of Deposit ☐ Safety Deposit Box

Institution _____

Address _____

Type _____

Account # _____

Owner _____

Value _____

This account is a: _____

Please indicate the type of account:

☐ Checking ☐ Savings ☐ Certificates of Deposit ☐ Safety Deposit Box

Total Value of Accounts: $ _____

Mutual Funds
For each mutual fund account, please attach a copy of your most recent statements.

Name of Broker _____

Type _____

Owner _____

Firm Name _____

Address of Firm _____

Phone _____

Account # _____

Amount _____

Name of Broker _____

Type _____

Owner _____

Firm Name _____

Address of Firm _____

Phone _____

Account # _____

Amount _____

Name of Broker _____

Type _____

Owner _____

Firm Name _____

Address of Firm _____

Phone _____

Account # _____

Amount _____

Name of Broker _____

Type _____

Owner _____

Firm Name _____

Address of Firm _____

Phone _____

Account # _____

Amount _____

Total Value: $ _____

Individual Stocks

Company Name _____

Owner _____

Number of Shares _____

Fair Market Value _____

Address _____

Phone _____

Certificate or Account Form _____

Company Name _____

Owner _____

Number of Shares _____

Fair Market Value _____

Address _____

Phone _____

Certificate or Account Form _____

Bond Number _____

Bond Serial Number _____

Institution/Type _____

Owner _____

Address _____

Phone _____

Bond Number _____

Bond Serial Number _____

Institution/Type _____

Owner _____

Address _____

Phone _____

Bond Number _____

Bond Serial Number _____

Institution/Type _____

Owner _____

Address _____

Phone _____

Bond Number _____

Bond Serial Number _____

Institution/Type _____

Owner _____

Address _____

Phone _____

Retirement Plans
Enter information about your pension plans, profit sharing plans, IRAs, 401(k), etc.

Name of Company _____

Type _____

Beneficiary upon your death _____

Value _____

Address _____

Phone _____

Name of Company _____

Type _____

Beneficiary upon your death _____

Value _____

Address _____

Phone _____

Life Insurance Policies

Enter details about your term, whole life, split dollar, and group life policies.

Name of Company _____

Type _____

Face Amount _____

Cash Value _____

Agent _____

Address _____

Phone _____

Policy Number _____

Insured _____

Owner _____

Primary Beneficiary _____

Secondary Beneficiary _____

Name of Company _____

Type _____

Face Amount _____

Cash Value _____

Agent _____

Address _____

Phone _____

Policy Number _____

Insured _____

Owner _____

Primary Beneficiary _____

Secondary Beneficiary _____

Name of Company _____

Type _____

Face Amount _____

Cash Value _____

Agent _____

Address _____

Phone _____

Policy Number _____

Insured _____

Owner _____

Primary Beneficiary _____

Secondary Beneficiary _____

Total Value: $ _____

Annuities

Name of Company _____

Face Amount_____

Cash Value_____

Account Number _____

Agent _____

Phone _____

Address _____

Insured _____

Annuitant _____

Primary Beneficiary _____

Secondary Beneficiary _____

Name of Company _____

Face Amount_____

Cash Value_____

Account Number _____

Agent _____

Phone _____

Address _____

Insured _____

Annuitant _____

Primary Beneficiary _____

Secondary Beneficiary _____

Total Value: $ _____

Mortgages, Notes & Other Receivables Owed to You
Enter information about mortgages or promissory notes, payable to you, as well as other monies owed to you. Please attach a copy of any promissory notes.

Name of Debtor _____

Due Date _____

Owed to _____

Current Balance _____

Name of Debtor _____

Due Date _____

Owed to _____

Current Balance _____

Name of Debtor _____

Due Date _____

Owed to _____

Current Balance _____

Total Value: $ _____

Partnership Interests

Provide information about any general and limited partnership interests you own. Please list the percentages that you own, and attach a copy of any partnership agreements.

_____

_____

_____

_____

_____

Corporate Business and Professional Interest

Name of Partnership _____

Owners _____

Value _____

Who holds partnership papers?_____

Phone _____

Name of Partnership _____

Owners _____

Value _____

Who holds partnership papers?_____

Phone _____

Total Value: $ _____

Please enter information about any privately owned (non-publicly traded) stock. Attach a copy of any Buy/Sell agreements, if applicable.

Company _____

Phone _____

Address _____

Number of Shares _____

Percent of Ownership _____

Is there a Buy/Sell Agreement? ☐ Yes ☐ No

Is there an S-Corporation? ☐ Yes ☐ No

Company _____

Phone _____

Address _____

Number of Shares _____

Percent of Ownership _____

Is there a Buy/Sell Agreement? ☐ Yes ☐ No

Is there an S-Corporation? ☐ Yes ☐ No

Sole Proprietorship, Business and Professsional Interests

Enter information about assets used by you in a sole proprietorship business.

Name of Business _____

Description of Business _____

Owner _____

Value _____

Name of Business _____

Description of Business _____

Owner _____

Value _____

Name of Business _____

Description of Business _____

Owner _____

Value _____

Total Value: $ _____

Oil, Gas, And Mineral Interests

Provide information about leases, overriding royalties, fee mineral estates, working interests, pooling agreements, etc. Please attach a copy of Agreement, Certificate of Deed.

Company _____

Type _____

Value _____

Address _____

Phone _____

County _____

Owner _____

Company _____

Type _____

Value _____

Address _____

Phone _____

County _____

Owner _____

Total Value: $ _____

Real Property

Describe land, buildings, homes and time-shares you own. Please attach a copy of the deed or agreement relating to each property.

Property _____

Fair Market Value _____

Address _____

Owner _____

County _____

Mortgage Company _____

Address of Mortgage Company _____

Loan Number _____

Property Casualty Insurance Company _____

Address _____

Homeowner's Policy Number _____

Property _____

Fair Market Value _____

Address _____

Owner _____

County _____

Mortgage Company _____

Address of Mortgage Company _____

Loan Number _____

Property Casualty Insurance Company _____

Address _____

Homeowner's Policy Number _____

Other Assets
Describe any property that you have that does not fit into any previous category.

Description _____

Owner _____

Value _____

Description _____

Owner _____

Value _____

Description _____

Owner _____

Value _____

Description _____

Owner _____

Value _____

Description _____

Owner _____

Value _____

Description _____

Owner _____

Value _____

Description _____

Owner _____

Value _____

Description _____

Owner _____

Value _____

Description _____

Owner _____

Value _____

Description _____

Owner _____

Value _____

Description _____

Owner _____

Value _____

Total Value: $ _____

Net Worth Summary
Total Assets

Primary Residence	Fair Market Value	$ _____
Other Real Property	Fair Market Value	$ _____
All Autos/Vehicles	Fair Market Value	$ _____
Stocks	Fair Market Value	$ _____
Mutual Funds	Fair Market Value	$ _____
Bonds	Fair Market Value	$ _____
Retirement Plans	Fair Market Value	$ _____
Life Insurance Policies	Cash Value	$ _____
Annuities	Cash Value	$ _____
Receivables	Cash Value	$ _____
Partnership Interests	Fair Market Value	$ _____
Oil, Gas & Mineral Interests	Fair Market Value	$ _____
Other Business Interests	Fair Market Value	$ _____
Other Assets	Fair Market Value	$ _____
	Total Assets:	$ _____

Total Liabilities

Mortgages	Current Balance	$ _____
Auto Loans	Current Balance	$ _____
Credit Cards	Current Balance	$ _____
Student Loans	Current Balance	$ _____
Other Debts	Current Balance	$ _____
	Total Liabilities:	$ _____

Net Worth

Total Assets $ _____

Less Total Liabilities $ _____

Net Worth: $ _____

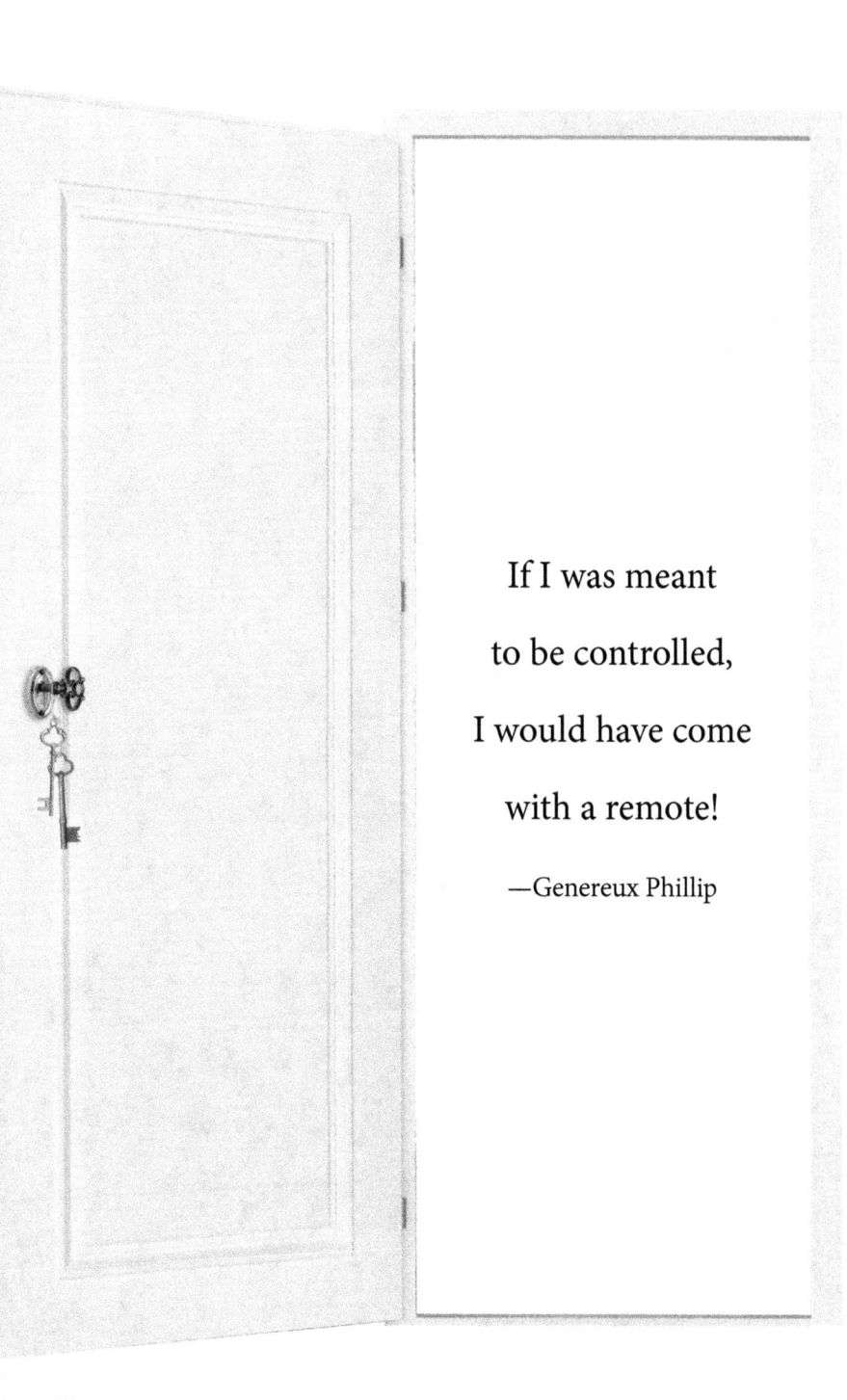

> If I was meant to be controlled, I would have come with a remote!
>
> —Genereux Phillip

Glossary

A

Abstract of Title A historical summary of all the recorded documents that affect the title of a property.

Acceleration Clause Language in a mortgage contract that allows the lender to demand that the entire mortgage be paid in full. The acceleration clause is usually triggered by a failure on the part of the borrower to live up to the contract, such as by missing mortgage payments.

Accrued Interest Interest earned over a specific period of time.

Acre A unit of measurement for land typically used to express the quantity of land upon which a home sits. One acre equals 43,560 square feet.

Addendum Something added as an attachment to a contract.

Adjustable Rate Mortgage (ARM) A type of mortgage that applies a variable interest rate to the mortgage principal, usually based on market conditions.

Adjusted Basis The original cost of the property increased by the value of any improvements and decreased by any depreciation.

Adverse Possession Ability of someone to take possession of a property away from the legal owner if the individual's possession of the land has been "actual, continues, hostile, visible, and distinct" for a period of time stated by law.

Air Rights Right to control the air space over a piece of property.

Air Space Space above a piece of property not occupied by a building.

Amortization Repayment of the mortgage loan over the term of years specified in the mortgage.

Amortization Schedule Table showing how much of the principal and how much of the interest is being repaid with each mortgage payment, as well as the balance of each that remains unpaid. It usually reflects the interest rate plus loan fees as though they were spread out over the term of the loan.

Annual Mortgage Statement A report from the lender that shows the amount of taxes, insurance, and interest paid during the past year, as well as the outstanding balance.

Annual Percentage Rate The effective rate of interest for a loan per year. Disclosure of the APR is required by the Truth in Lending law. It usually reflects the interest rate plus loan fees as though they were spread out over the term of the loan.

Apportionment A legal term for how real estate taxes, insurance premiums, and rents are divided between the buyer and the seller.

Appraisal A written analysis of a home's value, usually prepared by an independent third-party trained to conduct a thorough inspection of the home and assess its worth based on fair market value. Lenders require an appraisal to determine the amount of money they are willing to lend on a specific property.

Appraiser A trained professional who inspects a home or property and provides a written estimate of its value.

Appreciation The increase in the value of a home as a result of improvements, inflation, or other market conditions.

Appurtenance Something that is outside the property itself but is considered a part of the property and adds to its value (for example, an easement or right of way).

APR *see* Annual Percentage Rate

Architect's Inspection Certificate A document issued by an independent architect, verifying that a certain portion of construction on a project has been completed in accordance with approved plans and specifications.

ARM see Adjustable Rate Mortgage.

Arrears A term that refers to the end of the term. For example, annual property taxes are due at the end of the year. "Arrears" can also mean overdue.

Assessed Value The value of a home as determined by the tax assessor for the purpose of calculating annual property taxes

Assessor The government official who appraises a taxable property.

Asset Any property that has financial value.

Association Fee The fee imposed by a homeowner's association that has authority over a home, condominium, or townhome.

Assumable Mortgage A type of mortgage contract that may be transferred from one person to another.

Assumption of Mortgage The process of taking over the mortgage obligations of another borrower.

B

Balloon Mortgage A type of mortgage with low monthly payments until the final payment, due at the end of the term, and is typically very large.

Balloon Payment A payment on a mortgage that is larger than previous payments.

Bankruptcy A legal proceeding in federal court that allows a debtor to write off some or all of his or her debts. Recent changes in the federal bankruptcy law now require a debtor seeking bankruptcy protection to pass a means test. Depending on how much the debtor earns, he or she may he required to pay back part or all of the debt.

Beneficiary A person or entity that is the recipient of the proceeds or distributions from a trust, will, or estate.

Bill of Sale A legal document that transfers title to personal property from the seller to the buyer.

Bottom Ratio see Debt-to-Income Ratio

Bridge Loan A loan that arranges financing between the termination of one loan and the beginning of another. Can also be called a "gap" or "swing" loan.

Broker In the context of real estate, a person employed as an agent to bring buyers and sellers together.

Building Permit The written authorization from a local government authorizing construction of a building or extensive modifications to an existing structure.

Buy-Down Mortgage Money paid by the buyer of a house to reduce the monthly mortgage payments.

Buyer's Agent A real estate agent hired by a buyer to represent and advocate for him or her in the process of finding and buying a home.

Buyer's Market Economic conditions in which the supply of homes exceeds the number of buyers actively looking for a new home, giving the buyer the advantage when negotiating the selling price.

C

Cancellation Clause A provision in a contract that spells out the conditions under which each party to the contract can end the agreement.

Capital Improvement A major investment in a home that increases the home's value, such as a remodeled kitchen or room addition.

Capped Rate A commitment by a lender that locks in a maximum interest rate to which a loan can escalate.

Carry back Financing An agreement between buyer and seller in which the seller agrees to accept a note for a portion of the purchase price.

Certificate of Occupancy Written authorization from a local government that allows people to occupy a newly built or remodeled structure.

Chain of Title The history that goes back as far as records are available of conveyances and encumbrances affecting a title

Chapter 7 A type of bankruptcy proceeding which appoints a trustee who oversees the distribution of a debtor's assets to creditors.

Chapter 11 A type of bankruptcy case that allows a business to reorganize or discharge its debt obligations.

Chapter 13 A type of bankruptcy case that allows an individual to repay debt under more favorable conditions. The term is usually over a three- to five-year period.

Child Support A financial obligation the dissolution of a marriage required of one parent and payable to the other for the support of their child(ren).

Clear Title Title to property that has no liens or any legal encumbrances.

Closing A term that applies to the event that occurs at the end of the sale of property, usually attended by the buyer, seller, Realtor, and lender. During the closing, the loan documents are signed, the title is delivered, money is exchanged, and the buyer receives the keys to the home.

Closing Costs Various expenses and fees associated with the sale of a property and paid at the delivery of the deed.

Closing Statement A document commonly referred to as a Closing Disclosure that lists the final costs incurred to acquire financing and buy the house.

Cloud on Title An outstanding claim or encumbrance that, if valid, would affect or impair the owner's title.

Collateral An asset put up to guarantee that a loan will be repaid.

Commission Amount paid to a real estate broker for services performed.

Co-Mortgagee A second borrower who signs a mortgage loan with a mortgagor and who is jointly responsible for repayment of the loan.

Comparables Properties A list of properties that are similar to the one being sold or appraised.

Compound Interest Interest that is computed on both the original principal and accrued interest.

Condemnation A legal process of seizing private property for public use under the right of eminent domain, and for paying the legal owner of the property just compensation.

Condominium A form of property ownership whereby the buyer purchases title to a unit in a multi-unit structure as well as a portion of ownership in common areas.

Condominium Association Fees Fees paid by the homeowner to the association that governs a condominium development.

Condominium Conversion The process of converting rental properties with tenants into condominiums with owners.

Consideration Something of value offered and accepted in exchange for a promise, which is required for a contract to be valid and enforceable.

Construction Loan A short-term loan for financing the cost of construction of a building. Typically, the lender pays out portions of the loan to the borrower at specific intervals as construction progresses.

Consumer Credit Counseling Program A program that helps a consumer create a workable budget, reduce debts, and fix any past credit problems.

Contingency A condition that must be met before a contract can be enforced.

Contract to Purchase *see* Purchase and Sale Agreement

Contractor A person or company that agrees to perform work or provide materials for a contracted fee.

Conventional Financing Mortgage financing that isn't insured or guaranteed by a government agency.

Conventional Loan A mortgage that is not insured by FHA or VA.

Conversion Feature A feature of a mortgage that allows the conversion to another interest rate, mortgage term, or type of mortgage.

Convertible ARM A mortgage that has adjustable rates that can be converted to a fixed-rate mortgage upon fulfillment of certain conditions.

Convertible Mortgage Type of adjustable rate mortgage that may be converted to a fixed-rate mortgage.

Cooling-Off Period A period of time required by law or by contractual provisions during which one or both parties may legally back out of the transaction without repercussions.

Cooperative A form of multiple ownership in which a corporation or business entity holds title to a property and grants occupancy rights to tenants.

Co-Signer *see* Co-Mortgagee

Cost of Funds Index (COFI) An index based on the average yield paid by savings and loans on the funds they use to make mortgage loans.

Cost of Living Cost of the basic necessities of life.

Counter Proposal The response a seller makes to the buyer's offer.

Covenant The legal term for an enforceable promise or restriction written into deeds and other instruments agreeing to performance or non-performance of certain acts, or requiring or preventing certain uses of a property.

Credit Rating The rating given to a person, based on the individual's soft credit history, establishing his or her risk as a debtor.

Credit Report A professionally prepared report of an individual's past credit experience.

Credit Score A numerical value assigned to an individual by credit reporting agencies reflecting the likelihood that the individual will pay his or her bills.

Credit Worthiness A written analysis of an individual's credit risk as compared to other borrowers.

D

Debt-To-Income Ratio The percentage of an individual's income that must go to service debt and living expenses in relation to their gross or net income.

Deed A legal document that conveys title to a property.

Deed of Trust A document that is used in some states in mortgage documents to secure payment.

Default When a person fails to make payments on a mortgage or loan.

Depreciation A decline in the value of a property.

Discount Points Fees usually paid at the time of closing to lower the interest rate on a mortgage.

Down Payment The initial payment a buyer makes for a property, with the balance of payments coming from the mortgage loan or cash.

Documentary Stamp A mark or actual stamp put on a deed indicating that the proper transfer tax has seen paid.

Dual Agent A broker or agent who simultaneously acts as an agent for two individuals or entities. This is outlawed in some states.

Due-On-Sale Clause A legal clause in a mortgage contract that allows the lender to demand immediate payment of the balance of the mortgage when the borrower sells the home.

E

Earnest Money A payment of money that a potential buyer puts down along with his or her offer to show the seller that the buyer is serious.

Easement The right of way given to an individual or party other than the owner that allows access to the property.

Eighty-Ten-Ten Loan A combination of 80 percent loan to value first mortgage, a 10 percent second mortgage, and a 10 percent down payment. Another variation of this loan concept is the 80-15-5 loan. These loans eliminate the need for private mortgage insurance, which can increase the monthly cost of the mortgage.

Eminent Domain The government's right to seize private property for public use after fairly compensating the owner.

Encroachment An improvement or obstruction that physically intrudes, overlaps, or trespasses on someone else's property.

Encumbrance Any right or interest in a property that affects its value, such as outstanding liens, easements, or deed restrictions.

Environmental Impact Statement (EIS) A document required by many federal, state, and local land use laws that provides an analysis of the impact a proposed change may have on the environment of its locale.

Equal Credit Opportunity Act (ECOA) Federal law that requires all lenders to make credit equally available to credit-worthy individuals regardless of sex, race, age, religion, national origin, marital status, or receipt of income from public assistance.

Equity The value of a property less the current balance of the mortgage. Typically, the owner increases his or her equity in a property through mortgage payments, appreciation, or improvements.

Escrow An account held by a third party and used for such deposits as taxes, insurance, or earnest money. The money held in escrow is delivered to the intended party upon completion of contractual conditions, such as the purchase of a home.

Escrow Overage or Shortage The difference between funds held in escrow and funds required to make a payment when it becomes due.

Escrow Payment Portion of a mortgagee's monthly payments held by a lender in order to make payments for taxes and insurance when they become due.

Estate The assets owned by an individual.

Evidence of Title Proof of ownership of a property.

Examination of Title Review of the chain of title as discovered through an examination of the abstract of title or public record.

F

Fair Market Value The current price for which a property should sell, based on market conditions and what a buyer is willing to pay.

Fannie Mae (FNMA) The corporation created by the government that buys and sells conventional mortgages and mortgages that are insured by the FHA or VA.

Federal Housing Administration (FHA) A division of Housing and Urban Development that insures residential mortgage loans and sets standards for underwriting.

Federal Trade Commission (FTC) The government agency that monitors credit bureaus.

FHA Loan A loan insured by the Federal Housing Administration.

FHA Value The value established by the FHA as the basis for determining the maximum mortgage amount that may be insured on a specific property.

FICO A consumer's credit score developed by Fair Issac & Co. It is used by credit bureaus and credit-granting entities to determine the credit worthiness of an individual.

First Mortgage The mortgage taken out first in time, and which will be paid off first in a foreclosure.

Fixed-Rate Mortgage A mortgage with a fixed interest rate and payment amounts applied for the duration of the loan.

Fixture Any personal property that becomes a permanent part of the real estate. For example, curtain rods bolted to the wall or a chandelier mounted to the ceiling.

Flood Insurance Insurance for losses due to water damage. Depending on the property's location, flood insurance may be required by the lender.

Foreclosure The legal process by which a lender forces the sale of the property when the borrower fails to make mortgage payments.

Freddie Mac (FHLMC) Agency that purchases conventional mortgages from HUD-approved bankers.

G

Ginnie Mae (GNMA) Agency of the government that purchases conventional mortgages for HUD approved bankers.

Gross Monthly Income Total income received each month from every source before tax deductions and expenses.

Guaranteed Loan A loan that a government agency assures the lender will be paid back even if the borrower defaults.

H

Home Equity Line of Credit (HELOC) An open-ended loan, usually recorded as a second mortgage, that permits the borrower to obtain cash based on an approved amount with the home used as collateral.

Home Improvement Loan A mortgage to finance an addition to or rehabilitation of a residence.

Home Warranty A policy that provides repair or replacement for specific systems and appliances in the home while the policy is in force.

Homeowners Association (HOA) A group of owners who manage the common areas and set the rules homeowners must follow.

I

Improved Land A parcel of land that already has utilities, streets, sewers, other improvements.

Income/Expense Ratio The ratio, based on the borrower's income to expenses, used in underwriting a residential mortgage loan.

Income Property A property that is rented for money.

Index The rate used to compute the index on adjustable-rate mortgages.

Infrastructure A term that includes public services such as roads, sewers, water, drainage, and other utilities.

Installment Loan A loan that is paid in equal payments over a particular time period.

Insurance Binder A document written by an insurance company that states that temporary insurance is in effect.

Interest Rate Percentage paid for the use of money, usually expressed as an annual percentage.

Interest Rate Cap A limit on the interest rate increases or decreases during each interest rate adjustment or over the life of the mortgage.

Interim Financing A form of financing used from the beginning of a project to the closing of a permanent loan, usually part of a construction or development loan.

J

Joint Tenancy A type of legal ownership of property by two or more people, in which each owner owns an equal share of the property and has the rights of survivorship. For example, two joint tenants would each own 50 percent of the property.

L

Land Use Zones A zone in which local government ordinances dictate permitted land use.

Letter of Credit A letter from a lender authorizing a borrower to draw on a bank, or stating that the lender will provide the borrower with credit up to a specific amount.

Letter of Intent A letter from a buyer or developer stating interest in a property.

Lien A legal claim against a property that must be settled before the property can be sold.

Listing Agent A real estate agent who signs the contract with the seller to sell the property.

Loan The amount of money one person or entity allows another to borrow.

Loan Administration The lender's tasks associated with a loan, including the receipt of payments, customer service, escrow administration, investor accounting, collections, and foreclosures.

Loan Origination Procedures that a lender follows to issue a mortgage.

Loan Origination Fee The fee a lender charges a borrower for issuing a loan.

Loan Package A collection of documents associated with a specific loan application.

Loan Transfer The assumption of existing financing when an encumbered property is purchased by a new owner.

Lock In A written contract from a lender guaranteeing the borrower specific rates and loan terms for a period of time.

Long-Term Financing A loan with a term of ten or more years.

M

Maintenance Fee An assessment by a homeowner's association to pay the costs to operate or maintain the common elements in a development.

Market Value see Fair Market Value

Minimum Lot Zoning A zoning requirement that specifies the smallest lot site permitted per building.

Monthly Payment A payment comprised of principal and interest collected by lenders every calendar month. Monthly payments may also include escrow items such as property taxes and insurance.

Mortgage A loan for the purchase of property, with the property used as collateral to secure the loan.

Mortgage Banker An individual or company that exclusively lends money to borrowers purchasing property.

Mortgage Broker An individual who finds a mortgage for a buyer in exchange for a fee or commission.

Mortgage Commitment The agreement specifying the loan terms between a lender and borrower.

Mortgagee The person taking out the mortgage.

Mortgage Insurance An insurance contract that will pay the lender should the borrower default on the mortgage loan.

Mortgage Life Insurance The insurance policy that will pay the rest of the mortgage due if the primary borrower dies.

Multiple Listing Services (MLS) A service that provides information to members of a real estate association about every property that other members are selling.

N

National Association of Home Builders (NAHB) Trade association that provides lobbying and educational support to the building industry.

National Association of Mortgage Brokers (NAMB) An organization or professional society for mortgage brokers.

National Association of Realtors (NAR) Trade association representing real estate professionals.

Negative Amortization A scenario in which the principal balance of a loan increases rather than decreases because unpaid interest is added to the mortgage principal. This occurs when mortgage payments don't cover the full interest due.

Net Proceeds Amount of cash that the seller gets after expenses are deducted from the sale of a home.

Net Worth An accounting of the value of a person's assets less his or her debts.

Nonassumption Clause A provision in loan documents that prohibits a new borrower from assuming an existing loan.

Nonconforming Use The permitted use of real property that does not conform to current zoning laws.

Note The legal document that obligates a borrower to repay a debt.

Notice of Default A document sent to a defaulting party.

O

Offer The process of presenting the seller with the potential buyer's contractual expression of his or her desire to purchase the property.

Open Equity Line A second mortgage that is a fluctuating line of credit, with a balance that may rise and fall as the consumer draws against it or makes payments to it.

Option The right to purchase or lease a property with specified terms for a specified period of time.

Origination Date The date of the mortgage rate.

Origination Fee Charges assessed to a borrower to cover the costs of issuing a loan.

Owner Occupied Purchase The purchase of a property as the primary residence of the owner.

Owner Financing When the seller provides part or all of the financing in the sale of real estate.

P

Partial Entitlement The remaining dollar amount of a veteran's entitlement after the veteran has used part of his or her full entitlement of a VA mortgage.

Partial Payment A payment of only a portion of the required amount due, including payments received without the late charge.

Payment Cap A limitation on increases or decreases in the payment of an adjustable-rate or fixed-rate mortgage.

Payment History The part of a person's credit report that details on-time or late payments to creditors.

Pay Off Letter Statement detailing the unpaid principal balance, accrued interest, outstanding late charges, legal fees, and all other amounts necessary to pay off the lender in full.

Plat A map representing pieces of land subdivided into lots with streets, boundaries, easements, and legal dimensions indicated.

Plat Book The book of all maps within a specific geographic area.

Plot Plan A layout of improvements on a site, including their location, dimensions, and landscapes.

POC This stands for a charge that is paid outside of the closing.

Points The amount paid to the lender for processing the mortgage. One point is usually equal to one percent of the total mortgage amount.

Pre-Approved A process in which a lender approves a borrower for a certain loan amount. This requires a more thorough verification than a prequalification.

Prepayment Penalty Charge for paying off a mortgage ahead of time.

Prequalified The borrower has obtained preliminary approval for a loan. Final approval is not guaranteed.

Primary Residence A home that the owner occupies.

Prime Rate A specific interest rate that commercial banks charge their most credit-worthy clients for short-term loans.

Principal The amount of a loan, excluding interest.

Principal, Interest, Taxes, and Insurance (PITI) This represents the four components of a monthly mortgage payment.

Private Mortgage Insurance (PMI) The risk-management product that protects lenders against loss should a borrower default. It requires an additional charge to the mortgage payment.

Promissory Note A legal agreement to repay a certain amount of money.

Property Inspection A physical evaluation of a property to determine its condition.

Property Tax A tax imposed by a local government agency against the owner of real estate based on the value of the property. Property taxes are usually used to support local schools and infrastructure.

Pro Rate A method to divide or distribute a sum of money proportionately.

Purchase and Sale Agreement A written agreement between seller and purchaser in which they agree on certain terms and conditions for the transfer of the title from seller to purchaser.

Q

Qualification A process that determines whether an applicant can be approved for a mortgage loan.

Quiet Title Action A legal action taken to remove a defect regarding the legal rights of an owner to real property.

Quit Claim Deed A deed that conveys only the grantor's rights or interest in real estate with no warranties of ownership. This type of deed is frequently used in a divorce.

R

Radon A radioactive gas that may cause health problems and that is sometimes found in homes.

Ratio Method A calculation based on the consumer's income-to-debt that mortgage lenders use to determine how much the consumer can afford to borrow. That ratio varies from lender to lender.

Real Estate A term used to describe land with or without buildings on it.

Real Estate Agent A professional licensed by the state and authorized to assist in the sale or purchase of real estate.

Real Estate Attorney A legal professional who specializes in real estate law.

Real Estate Broker A state licensed agent who, for a fee, acts for individuals in real estate transactions within the scope of state law.

Real Estate Taxes Local government fees levied annually on the ownership of real estate.

Reassessment The revaluation of property for tax purposes.

Real Property The legal name for the home, the land, other permanent structures and all other rights included in the property.

Realtor® A real estate professional who has obtained membership in a local real estate board affiliated with the National Association for Realtors.®

Recordation Fees The fees charged by a local government to record the documents involved in a real estate transaction.

Recorder The public official who legally records the deed after the property has been sold or transferred.

Recording A system of filing a legal document, usually with the county, to provide a traceable chain of title to the *property*.

Regulation Z The regulation written by the Federal Reserve Board to implement the Truth in Lending Act, requiring full written disclosure of the credit portion of a purchase including the annual percentage rate.

Regulatory Agency The arm of the state or federal government that has the responsibility to license, pass laws, regulate, audit and monitor industry related issues.

Rehabilitation Loan The term used by some lenders for a loan that replaces a defaulted loan and clears up the bad credit history the default reflects.

Reinstatement Action taken by a lender after a borrower brings a loan current by making up missed payments.

Release Discharge of secured property after a lien is satisfied.

Release of Liability A written method used by a lender to terminate the personal obligation of a mortgagee in connection with payment of a debt.

Release of Lien The document that discharges a secured property from a lien.

Release Price The amount of money that must be paid to remove a lien from a specific property.

Rent with Option To Buy An agreement between the owner of a property and potential buyer in which the buyer may be allowed to apply part or all of rent paid toward the down payment on the purchase of the property within a specific time period.

Replacement Cost The cost to replace a structure with one of an equal though not necessarily identical value and function.

Restrictive Covenant A restrictive covenant is a clause in a deed or lease to real property that limits what the owner of the land or lease can do with the property.

Retirement Community A planned community designed to meet the needs of individuals of retirement age.

Return On Investment (ROI) The percent of profit earned in relation to the original amount invested.

Revolving Credit A line of credit with variable payments that reflect the current balance.

Rider An added clause to a contract.

Right of First Refusal A right given by an owner to another individual by which the owner grants the individual the first right to purchase a specific property. It may contain contingencies.

Right of Ingress or Egress The right to enter or leave a portion of the property.

Right of Redemption A right in some states that permits the owner to reclaim foreclosed property upon making full payment of the foreclosed sales price within a specific time period.

Right of Survivorship A feature of joint tenancy, this right allows a surviving joint tenant to immediately inherit the deceased tenant's ownership share in a property without probate.

Right of Way The right to traverse across land owned by another.

Riparian Rights The rights of owners to the water and land within the normal flow of a river or stream, below a high water mark. These rights vary from state to state.

S

Sale-Buyback Financing arrangement where a developer sells a property to an investor, then buys it back on a long-term contract.

Sale-Leaseback A sales arrangement in which a seller deeds a property to a buyer for consideration. The seller then leases the same property back from the buyer.

Sales Contract A written agreement between the buyer and seller specifying the terms of a sale of property.

Seasoned Mortgage A mortgage on which payments have been made regularly for at least one year.

Secondary Market A system where home loans and servicing rights are bought and sold between lenders and investors

Secured Loan A loan which is secured by collateral, such as real estate.

Seller's Agent The real estate agent who represents the seller of property.

Senior Mortgage Another term for a first mortgage

Settlement Another term for the closing.

Settlement Costs Expenses paid by the buyer and seller to achieve the closing. Expenses include fees for the insurance, survey, attorney's fees, and Realtor® commissions.

Sheriff's Deed A deed given by court order when a property is sold to satisfy a judgment or tax lien.

Site Plan A drawing that shows all improvements to be made to a site, such as grading, clearing and installation of utilities.

Special Assessment District A government-created subdivision with the power to tax and improve property within its jurisdiction.

Special Warranty Deed A deed containing a covenant whereby the grantor agrees to protect the grantee against any claims arising during the grantor's period of ownership.

Strict Foreclosure A type of foreclosure in which title to the foreclosed property is invested directly in the mortgagor by court decree without holding a foreclosure sale. This process varies by state.

Student Loan A loan usually backed by the government, that a student takes out to finance his or her higher education.

Subcontractor A person or company contracted to perform work for a developer or general contractor.

Subdivision An area of land that is divided into parcels for sale, lease or development.

Subsurface Rights The ownership rights to everything below ground, such as oil or minerals.

Superior Lien A lien or encumbrance that takes priority over other liens of encumbrances.

Survey The process by which a parcel of land is measured and its area ascertained.

Surveyor's Certificate A formal statement that is signed, dated, and certified by a registered surveyor, and that gives the pertinent facts about a piece of property.

T

Take-Home Pay The borrower's paycheck after taxes and other deductions have been subtracted.

Tax Deduction The amount the state or federal government allows you to subtract from your income before your tax liability is calculated.

Tax Deed The deed on property purchased at a public sale for nonpayment of taxes.

Tax Lien A claim against property for unpaid taxes.

Tax Sale A sale of property by a taxing authority acting on a judgment for back taxes.

Tenancy by the Entirety allows spouses to own property together as a single legal entity. Under a tenancy by the entirety, creditors of an individual spouse may not attach and sell the interest of a debtor spouse: only creditors of the couple may attach and sell the interest in the property owned by tenancy by the entirety.

Tenancy In Common A title to property in which owners do not necessarily have equal shares and do not have the right to survivorship.

Term A period of time, usually slated in months or years needed to repay a mortgage.

Title The document that shows the current legal owner of a property.

Title Company A company that sells title insurance.

Title Exception The exception that appears on a title insurance policy against which the insurance company will not insure.

Title Insurance Commitment A document that provides assurance that a title company will provide a title insurance policy for a specific property.

Title Insurance Policy A contract by which the insurer agrees to pay the insured a specific sum for any loss caused by defects of title to real estate.

Title Search A check of records to determine who owned the property and what liens have been placed on the property from the time the property was built.

Total Expense Ratio When applied to a mortgage scenario it is a person's debt as a percentage of his or her gross income.

Townhouse A dwelling unit, usually having two or more floors and attached to similar units by virtue of a shared wall.

Tract A parcel of land.

Treasury Index A type of index used in ARMs and based on auctions conducted by the U.S. Treasury for Bills and Securities.

Truth in Lending see Regulation Z.

U

Underwriting A review process conducted by an underwriter to evaluate a loan application.

Unencumbered Property A property free and clear of any debts, liens or judgments.

Unsecured Loan A loan that isn't backed by collateral.

Usury Charging a borrower an interest rate greater than that allowed by law.

Usury Ceiling A maximum interest rate allowed by law that lenders may charge borrowers for the use of money.

Utilities Basic services associated with developed areas, such as electricity, gas, telephone, sewer, and garbage collection.

V

VA Loan Mortgage loan made by an approved lender and guaranteed by the Department of Veterans Affairs.

Vested Usually used to indicate the percentage of ownership that an employee has in his or her retirement account.

Valuation An estimate of a property's value determined by an appraisal.

Variable Rate Mortgage (VRM) see Adjustable Rate Mortgage.

Variance The approved special change in construction codes, zoning requirements or other property restrictions.

Verification of Employment (VOE) A form lenders use to verify a borrower's current employment.

Verification of Mortgage A form lenders use to obtain the history of a potential borrower's payments on his or her current mortgage.

Void A term used in real estate, most commonly as, "null and void," that means, "no longer in effect."

W

W-2 An IRS form that reports a worker's income paid as well as the taxes paid during a calendar year.

W-4 An IRS form that shows the amount of federal taxes the employer will withhold from the worker's paycheck during each pay period.

Waiver A legal document that gives an individual permission to avoid or take a specific action that would otherwise be required.

Warranty A guarantee that will cover repairs or replacement to certain features of a home if they are defective: for example the appliances or systems in the home.

Will A legal document that allows a person to distribute his or her assets after death.

Wraparound Mortgage An additional mortgage that includes payments made on prior mortgages.

Z

Zero-Down Mortgages A mortgage that allows the borrower to finance 100 percent of the home's selling price.

Zero Lot Line The positioning of a structure on a lot so that one side sits directly on the lot's boundary line.

Zoning The process by which local governments create districts and authorize how specific types of properties may be used.

Zoning Regulations The laws enacted by governments that dictate how specific types of properties may be used.

Resources

Recommended Books/Articles

The Divorce Revolution, Lenore J. Weitzman (Free Press, 1985)

The Good Divorce, Constance Ahrons (William Morrow Paperbacks, 1995)

Collaborative Divorce: A New Paradigm, Pauline H. Tesler and Peggy Thompson (HarperCollins, 2009)

The Gray Divorce Revolution: Rising Divorce among Middle-aged and Older Adults, 1990-2010, Susan Brown and I-Fen Lin (National Center for Family & Marriage Research, 2013)

Your Money or Your Life: 9 Steps to Transforming Your Relationship with Money and Achieving Financial Independence, Vicki Robin and Joe Dominguez (Penguin Books, 2008)

Divorce & Money: How to Make the Best Financial Decisions During Divorce, Matthew J. Perry and Violet Woodhouse (NOLO, 2013)

Financial advantages to owning your own home: http://www.ginniemae.gov/rent_vs_buy/rent_vs_buy_calc.asp?section=Search

Money Management Programs

- Quicken from Intuit
- www.mint.com
- www.moneydance.com/
- www.mvelopes.com
- www.budgetpulse.com

Mortgage Resources

- Government Loan and Conventional Loan Comparison *http://www.nolo.com/legal-encyclopedia/what-the-difference-between-conventional-fha-va-loan.html*
- FHA Loans *www.fha.com*
- Reverse Mortgages *https://www.consumer.ftc.gov/articles/0192-reverse-mortgages*
- VA Loans *http://www.benefits.va.gov/homeloans/*
- Federal National Mortgage Association (Fannie Mae) *www.fanniemae.com/portal/index.html*
- Federal Home Mortgage Corporation (Freddie Mac) *www.freddiemac.com*
- Loan fees information *http://www.consumerfinance.gov/know-before-you-owe/*

Items to Gather When Preparing to File for Divorce

- Last Will and Testament
- Social Security Card, driver's license, and other identification cards
- Discharge papers and VA claim number, if applicable
- Marriage and birth certificates
- All insurance policies
- Deeds and titles to all real estate properties
- Recent tax forms and W-2s (three years, if possible)
- Mortgage and other loan information
- Statements of financial accounts, including all account numbers
- All business and legal agreements

- Monthly bills, checkbooks, and credit cards
- Safe deposit box information

Home Warranty Companies
Companies offering home warranties *https://www.consumersadvocate.org/home-warranties/best-home-warranties*

Tax Requirements
- IRS Tax Publications: https://www.irs.gov/publications/
  - 936 Home Mortgage Interest Deduction
  - 521 Moving Expenses
  - 523 Selling Your Home
  - 908 Bankruptcy Tax Guide
  - 530 First Time Homebuyers

Credit Reporting Agencies
- Equifax *www.econsumer.equifax.com*
- Experian *www.experian.com/consumer*
- Transunion *www.transunion.com/consumer*
- Free Annual Credit Report *www.annualcreditreport.com*
- Credit Information Resources *www.creditkarma.com www.scoreinfo.org*

Credit Counseling
- National Foundation for Credit Counseling *https://www.nfcc.org*

National Real Estate Information Exchanges
- *Realtor.com®*
- *Experian.com*
- *Zillow.com*
- *Trulia.com*
- *Yahoo.com*

Consumer Protection
- Consumer Financial Protection Bureau *http://www.consumerfinance.gov/*

Acknowledgments

The inspiration and motivation for *Your Keys to Moving On* came from the thousands of women who have shared their stories. They knew this book would provide a trusted resource for anyone navigating the thorny life decisions around divorce.

Just as divorce takes a team, so does writing a book, and my thanks go to my team.

Kelly Johnson, my team leader in this endeavor, continually offered her gentle guidance and years of experience. She connected me with Rebecca Finkel, a masterful designer, and Barbara McNichol, a stellar editor.

Thanks in abundance to my two children Doug and Jennifer who have made this divorce journey with me. They were always there to cheer me on with their wisdom, insight, and wry senses of humor!

Wildflower Group

Joan Rogliano created Wildflower Group in 2006 to empower women facing divorce and widowhood. This book is a result of her vast experience with this topic gained through her real estate career and Wildflower Group.

Wildflower Group is now operating in ten states and was featured on the *TODAY* show. Joan and the organization were profiled for the work they are doing on behalf of divorcing women who are frequently bullied or intimidated into making decisions that are not in their best interest.

Please contact Joan at *joan@wildflowergroup.net* to book her as a speaker on the topic of women and divorce. Visit *www.wildflowergroup.net* for divorce resources and to find a Wildflower Group near you.

One of the Nation's most highly trained and experienced Realtors, **Joan Rogliano** holds advanced certifications as a Certified Real Estate Divorce Specialist, a Certified Luxury Home Marketing Specialist (CLHMS), Council of Residential Specialist (CRS), and Graduate of the Real Estate Institute (GRI).

As a Real Estate Divorce Specialist, she joins lawyers, accountants, and other advisors as part of a team which guides families through the web of tax and legal implications when dividing or liquidating real estate.

"With the right information and a collaborative team, it is possible to diffuse conflict for families. The family home is usually the source of a lot of emotion and the largest financial investment most people make. The decision of what to do with the property must be made from an informed place," said Rogliano.

Ms. Rogliano was featured on the *TODAY* show for her continued work with families navigating divorce.

Please contact *Joan@RoglianoRealEsateGroup.com*.

www.ingramcontent.com/pod-product-compliance
Lightning Source LLC
Chambersburg PA
CBHW050540300426
44113CB00012B/2189